Torn Curtain Publishing
Wellington, New Zealand
www.torncurtainpublishing.com

© Copyright 2022 Amber Johnson. All rights reserved.

ISBN Softcover 978-0-6453977-0-3

No portion of this book may be reproduced, stored in a retrieval system or transmitted in any form or by any means—electronic, mechanical, photocopy, recording or otherwise—except for brief quotations in printed reviews of promotion, without prior written permission from the author.

Unless otherwise noted, all scripture is taken from the ESV® Bible (The Holy Bible, English Standard Version®), copyright © 2001 by Crossway, a publishing ministry of Good News Publishers. Used by permission. All rights reserved.

Scripture quotations marked NKJV are taken from the New King James Version. Copyright © 1982 by Thomas Nelson, Inc. Used by permission. All rights reserved.

Scripture quotations marked AMP are taken from the Amplified® Bible (AMPC), Copyright © 1954, 1958, 1962, 1964, 1965, 1987 by The Lockman Foundation. Used by permission. www.lockman.org.

Scripture quotations marked NLT are taken from the Holy Bible, New Living Translation, copyright © 1996, 2004, 2015 by Tyndale House Foundation. Used by permission of Tyndale House Publishers, Inc., Carol Stream, Illinois 60188. All rights reserved.

Scripture quotations marked TPT are from The Passion Translation®. Copyright © 2017, 2018, 2020 by Passion & Fire Ministries, Inc. Used by permission. All rights reserved. ThePassionTranslation.com.

Scripture quotations marked KJV are from The Authorized (King James) Version. Rights in the Authorized Version in the United Kingdom are vested in the Crown. Reproduced by permission of the Crown's patentee, Cambridge University Press.

Cover art by Nathan McGregor. Used with permission.
Crown by Icon Producer from the Noun Project.

Cataloging in Publishing Data
  Title: You Are Powerful
  Author: Amber Johnson
  Subjects: Christian living, Calling and vocation, Spiritual Growth, Women's Interests

You Are
POWERFUL

Embracing the Woman of Power and
Purpose God Created You to Be

Amber N Johnson MD

Dedication

To every woman holding this book. May you be touched by the love of God and transformed by His magnificent grace into the powerful woman of Kingdom destiny He sees inside of you. I pray the Lord speaks through the pages of this book and beyond to introduce you to the woman you truly are; she is a true woman of valor and I can't wait for you to meet her.

To the friends who have become more like sisters in this season: Laura Hubers, Melissa Louhisdon, and Shannon O'Donnell. Thank you for walking by my side, encouraging me, and building me up through one of the toughest seasons of my life (the backdrop for the revelations contained in this book), for showing me what it means to be a Kingdom woman, and for believing in me when I don't have the strength to believe for myself. You each uniquely and beautifully embody what it is to be a woman of power and purpose, and have impacted my life so much more than you know.

To God my Redeemer, King, and Friend. Thank you for relentlessly pursuing my heart, for teaching me what it is to be a woman, for speaking truth and identity over me, and for never giving up on me. Words cannot convey my gratitude for the victorious love of the Father, the empowering grace of Jesus, and the sweet friendship of Holy Spirit. I will never stop pursuing You with all my heart.

Foreword

by Hayley Braun

Women, we are called to be powerful, deeply loved daughters, re-presenting God to the world in the unique way only we can. When this revelation grabs hold of you, everything changes!

Amber Johnson's personal journey as a single woman working in the medical field, is one of discovering these truths and moving into real freedom and God-given destiny.

I have met many women who have struggled with grasping their value and the strength within their femininity—women who felt like they were relegated to places "less than", or held to expectations that were simply impossible to meet.

In this book, Amber vulnerably invites you into her own story and personal journey. Join her as she dives into Proverbs 31, a chapter that for years has felt unrelatable and unattainable to many. Pulling from history, Amber expands on the virtues of the Proverbs 31 woman by looking to other female heroes in the Bible: Lydia, Ruth, and Esther.

Whether you are single or married, young or old, have your own children or not, this passage will speak to you as a woman in fresh ways. Not only will you find yourself in it, you will find what it looks like to be a world changing woman! You will discover that this is not dependent on your station in life, but is rooted in your character and who God calls you to be. Amber's journey will unmask lies and shed light on God's powerful design for women. The journey has no shortcuts, but involves deep heart work, allowing God to do all that He wants in order to free and transform us. You will be challenged and invited to let God do this work in you.

I pray that through this book you will be met powerfully by the precious Holy Spirit, and that he will lead you into the radical truth of who God calls you to be and how it is all made possible in Jesus through the price He paid.

Contents

    Introduction   *1*

1. **Purity:** *Inviting Divine Presence, Purpose, and Protection*   *7*
2. **Prayer:** *Partnering with God*   *23*
3. **Peace:** *The Pace of Abiding*   *39*
4. **Perception:** *The Spiritual Power of Woman's Intuition*   *55*
5. **Provision:** *Creating Strong Foundations*   *69*
6. **Protection:** *Guarding Spiritual Families*   *81*
7. **Prophetic Processing:** *The Destiny-Releasing Power of Woman*   *97*
8. **Power and Purpose:** *Putting it All Together*   *113*

    Epilogue   *127*

Introduction

Women are powerful. I have not always believed that. For most of my life, I did not consider it a good thing to be female and even resented being created a woman, secretly feeling that God must have had something against me. Womanhood seemed to come with a whole host of disadvantages and restrictions and limitations in the form of domestic demands and expectations.

The realization that I resented my own womanhood surprised me. I was a practicing physician and was continuing to receive wholehearted encouragement from my family with regard to my medical career. At least on a surface level, it seemed my position as a female physician should have proven to me that in twenty-first century America, being a woman is not a disadvantage. The problem was that I still considered being a woman to be a negative. As I reflected on where this deeply-rooted belief came from, figuring there must have been something from culture or past relationships that sparked this idea in me, I knew the issue went much farther back and much deeper in my heart than any of the people or situations I tried to blame.

It wasn't until recently while speaking with a friend who told me about a restricted view of womanhood voiced by her thirteen-year-old daughter that I recognized a lie I had come into agreement with at a very young age. My friend, who is also a physician, was alarmed by her daughter's statements which largely centered around the idea that a woman's primary purpose is to please and serve her man.

This was very similar to the false beliefs I had been struggling to sort through in my own heart. The crazy thing was that neither my friend's daughter nor I grew up in a home environment that taught anything of the sort, yet we both had a mysteriously deeply-rooted false understanding of what it is to be a woman.

I had felt called by God to be a doctor, but somehow, I believed that my life as a single female physician contradicted the biblical expectations and definitions of womanhood. Because I could not reconcile the two seemingly contradictory identities, I chose to resent my womanhood in order to make me feel comfortable both with my singleness and with my career as a doctor.

But the thing that throws a wrench in that whole line of thinking is this: *God values women.*

God saw the value of women long before we lost sight of it. He values us so much that He made a point to call us out as the unique and powerful beings we are before we were even created. In the midst of bringing life to His most important and beloved masterpiece, God paused to make a dramatic declaration: "It is not good that man should be alone" (Genesis 2:18). God saw that creation was not complete without women, that the universe *needed* the unique calling inherent in women. Without it, earth would never be brought under the governance of His Kingdom the way He intended.

I believe the Enemy took that declaration and from the moment woman was created, launched a vicious attack against her strength, identity, and purpose. The devil understands the power of women and is intent on aligning our hearts with a false concept of what it is to be a woman so that he can effectively repress our scope and impact. In Genesis 3:15, God told the devil that because he made the mistake of picking a fight with Eve, womankind became his 'forever enemy'.

The devil targeted us in Eden and has been after us ever since because he knows the force we are. It is time we realized our power too—time

INTRODUCTION

we stepped up from the ashes of everything the Enemy has tried to set fire to, and ask our Redeemer-King to turn ashes into beauty.

The reality is that God has deposited something in the spirit of woman that the world is in desperate need of. We reflect the Lord's nature in a way that is beautifully distinct from the way God created men to reflect Him. If we abdicate that responsibility and do not own and express the unique ways the Lord created us to depict His nature, the world will have only half the representation of who He is manifested in humanity. The revelation that rocked my world and set me free from the internal crisis of striving to live out two seemingly opposing identities was the realization that my idea of womanhood was completely wrong. Until then, I struggled with the concept of womanhood in Proverbs 31. The description King Solomon gives there of a godly woman seemed unrealistic and unattainable, and if I'm being honest as a single woman, unrelatable.

> **God has deposited something in the spirit of woman that the world is in desperate need of.**

Over this past year however, as the Lord has been uprooting false beliefs in my heart about womanhood and revealing the uniquely powerful ways He equipped women with spiritual gifts, anointings, and assignments that contribute to the world and reflect His glory in ways that are needed and are distinct from the way He equipped men, I came to fall in love with Proverbs 31. I began looking deeper at the godly woman Solomon describes. I began to perceive the spiritual truths behind the account of her day-to-day life, realizing for example that what we read of her career exploits speaks to her work ethic and creativity, while descriptions of her relationship with her husband testify more to her *character* as a trustworthy, faithful woman than to her marital status. When I realized I didn't have to model her exact schedule and that I didn't have to wait to have a husband before I could start living my life as a Proverbs 31 woman, I developed a desire to study and get to know the character of this woman.

What I found, was a woman at rest in her God-given identity as a woman of "virtue" or literally "valor" (Proverbs 31:10). Such a strong word might not be the first that comes to mind for us if asked to describe women, but it is the one God's Spirit inspired King Solomon to write.

> "She equips herself with strength [spiritual, mental, and physical fitness for her God-given task] And makes her arms strong."
>
> Proverbs 31:17 AMP

The truth is, the world *needs* women who lead and influence in the way women were wired to lead and influence. I believe in this season, God is inviting His daughters to return to places of honor, and to own their unique places of authority and influence. He is inviting us to recognize our identity and realize our destinies. He is inviting us to run after life with arms wide open and head held high. He is inviting us to own our identity specifically as *women* made in His image and for His glory and equipped with unique purpose, gifting, and destiny.

The world needs women who lead and influence in the way women were wired to lead and influence.

The more I discover how He sees me and who it is He created me to be, the more I am blown away by the unique power we carry and the unique place we as daughters hold in our Father's heart. History is full of women God raised up at the opportune time to take on an assignment uniquely tailored to a woman's touch. Deborah empowered an army. Mary mothered the Messiah. Esther saved her people from destruction. Lydia birthed the Philippian church. Now it is our time to rise.

My prayer is that the Lord would speak to you through the pages of this book. I pray that He would start a conversation with you about life and truth and identity and purpose, about who He is and who you are in Him.

INTRODUCTION

I invite you to journey with me as we rediscover *woman* as God created her to be, to rediscover our unique giftings, callings, and identities so that, walking in the strength, might, and power of our womanhood, we can give the world back the weapon God intended us to be.

> "Who can find a virtuous woman? For her price is far above rubies." Proverbs 31:10 KJV

Purity

Inviting Divine Presence, Purpose, and Protection

Purity is under attack. More specifically (or more vulnerably), *my* purity is under attack. In what has been the most refining and defining season of my life to date, the Enemy specifically targeted my purity—with the aim of destroying my belief that my purity could ever be restored. The attack began with a series of events in which two things happened. I was taken advantage of by someone I respected, and I chose to compromise myself and give in to sin. Together, the betrayal by someone I deeply trusted and the reality of my own sin sent me into months of the deepest shame I have ever experienced. In my mind, this was a season that had no end and I could never be free from the shame. Caught in a seemingly endless cycle of repentance, I felt that not only had my purity been stolen, but that I could never again be pure in God's eyes. And yet the Lord kept breaking through my tears of self-condemnation with a simple question: "Amber, do you believe in the power of redemption?"

In the same way Jesus asked Peter over and over again, "Do you love me?" (John 21:15-17), He kept asking me that question: "Do you believe in the power of redemption?"—because the truth was, I didn't believe it. I believed restoration was possible for everyone else, but not for me. I didn't believe He could redeem me or that His grace was strong enough for me. I felt that because of what happened and what I did, the only way forward was to prove myself once again. I was convinced I needed to earn my own redemption.

What I didn't realize was that purity cannot be stolen, and it is never irretrievably lost! No matter how much my self-condemnation made me believe He would be better off without me, the Lord refused to give up. He knew that the power of redemption is stronger than the power of sin and shame, and He was relentless in His pursuit to bring my heart into alignment with His truth about my purity.

Purity Defined

Purity is essentially a matter of the heart (see James 4:8 and Matthew 5:8). Our 'hearts' are who we are at the deepest core of our being, and to be pure in heart is to long for and be motivated by Jesus alone. The Lord says of His people in Jeremiah 32:39, "I will give them one heart and one way, that they may fear me forever." Being 'pure of heart' means the Lord is the single desire with which we are consumed.

A pure heart places us in a right relationship with God; it opens doors to the presence of God and to the fullness of His callings for us (Psalm 24:3-4). Because of this, our adversary the devil has been on mission to destroy our understanding of what purity is as well as our understanding of how to obtain purity. I believe in this season the Lord is on mission to rebuke the lies the Enemy has spoken over His daughters in this area so that He can lead our hearts to believe in the power of His redemption to

The devil has been on mission to destroy our understanding of what purity is.

restore and maintain our purity.

The first descriptive adjective King Solomon uses to describe the woman living out the fullness of her call to womanhood in Proverbs 31 is "virtuous". In Hebrew, the word is *chayil*, and its literal translation is "strength, efficiency, wealth". It is the same Hebrew word translated "valor" when used to describe men of war and in the specific context of verse 10 of Proverbs 31 it carries the connotation of "ability, efficiency, often involving moral worth" (Brown et al, 1996).

How interesting that the first word Solomon chooses to describe the Proverbs 31 woman denotes both the strength of a mighty army (valor) and the strength inherent in good moral character (virtue)! To be strong in character is to carry the strength of a mighty army and as warriors in God's Kingdom, the army we fight is not a physical one but a spiritual one comprised of demonic systems under the rule of the devil (Ephesians 6:12).

As the highest version of strong moral character, purity is inherently tied to the "virtue" Solomon describes as the sought-after characteristic of a godly woman. Vine's Expository Dictionary describes purity as "pure from defilement; not contaminated". To *be pure* is to be comprised of a single substance with no contributions or "contamination" from other substances. Pure water is water that is comprised of only water with no other substances in it, pure gold is gold that is comprised of only gold with no other substances, and pure people are people who are filled with only God and nothing else.

Purity is a Who not a What

Purity is a matter of character. It is not a matter of what you have or haven't done; it isn't diminished by mistakes we have made or enhanced by our graces. Since purity is a character trait, it is a part of *who* you are, not *what* you do. This is so important because the Enemy loves to tell us that *what* we have done or *what* we've been labeled as makes purity beyond our grasp. But this is simply not true. What you may have done (or not done) does not revoke your purity. Jesus is the one who makes us pure, and He does this by transforming our very nature, changing *who* we are. The Lord promises in Ezekiel 36:26, "I will give you a new heart, and a new spirit I will put within you."

Purity is a matter of who you are, not what you do.

What you do is fleeting, limited by time and space. But who you are is eternal. You will not always be characterized by *what* you do today, but you will always be *who* you are.

Twenty thousand years from now, when this present world is overshadowed by new realities and we are walking out even higher eternal destinies in new dimensions with Jesus and what you've done is long forgotten, you will still be who you are, because who you are is eternal.

Daughters of the King, hear this: Purity is who you are. And who you are is eternal. When you allowed Jesus to wash you clean by taking your place and absolving the debts that separated you from the Father, you became pure in His sight. Nothing can take that away. The consequence of past, present, and future sin is swallowed up in victory. It doesn't matter what you did yesterday, or what you might do tomorrow—they will never change who you are.

> *"Therefore, if anyone is in Christ, [she] is a new creation. The old has passed away; behold the new has come."*
>
> *1 Corinthians 5:17*

This isn't to say we will never compromise, or that we are immune to the Enemy's devices, but as those who have become daughters of the King through faith in Jesus, the essence of who we are does not change, no matter what we succumb to post-redemption. As sinners transformed into saints through His saving grace, we are clothed in the righteousness of Jesus (Isaiah 61:10), and our righteousness is no longer dependent on our works, but instead dependent only on the completed, perfect work of Jesus.

So what happens when we do fall—when we compromise sexually or emotionally? When we fall into sin or moral compromise, we do not negate the work Jesus has done in our hearts, but we introduce another substance into our hearts and lives, one that distracts and subtracts from our singleness of heart. Our purity is not irretrievable and we are still redeemed, but our pure-hearted devotion to Christ is compromised.

Allowing our hearts to be divided incapacitates our purity so that it cannot protect us and empower us the way it is meant to. But there is good news! Mixed-in substances are easily removed by the filter of God's grace. Repenting—which means recognizing we are going in the wrong direction and stopping what we are doing so we can run back to Jesus as our true source of fulfillment and joy—is an instantaneous filter-establishing decision.

For some of us, the contaminating situations we fear have taken our purity were not the result of our own decisions, but were imposed on us by someone else. Abuse (and particularly sexual abuse) is rampant and tragically, many of us continue to go about life thinking we are the only ones carrying these scars when the reality is that so many of the people we come across in everyday situations, including very likely many of the people we have known and called friends for years, are also carrying the scars of abuse while similarly believing they are the only ones. Fellow women of purity, please let this truth cut through to your heart: Your purity cannot be stolen. Remember, purity is a character trait, and character is not something that can be stolen. When that individual manipulated you into giving your body in a way you didn't want to, they hurt you deeply, but they did not steal your purity. In Christ, we are a new creation (2 Corinthians 5:17) and nothing can steal our purity because nothing can steal *who we are*.

Purity is our identity, first as His children who have been washed clean through Jesus' death for us, but also and more specifically as His daughters because the description of a godly woman, according to the wisdom with which King Solomon wrote of her, is that she is "a woman of virtue."

The Enemy wants you to believe you are not pure and can never be pure. Reject his lies! The devil is the father of lies, and anything he tells you is guaranteed to be a lie, or at best (possibly worse!) a half-truth. So, when he tells us anything about our purity, we must recognize the motivation behind his schemes—the devil is terrified of our purity.

Our Enemy knows the kingdom-advancement that is activated when women step into the purity-carrying assignment God gave them. The reason emotional and sexual abuse are so rampant, and the reason guilt and condemnation of past sins often have such a death-grip hold on us is that the Enemy wants to distort our understanding of purity and suppress our ability to release it as the weapon it is.

With that in mind, let's dive into the truth about the power of woman's purity.

Inviting Divine Presence

One of the reasons God entrusted His daughters to carry such an important gift as purity is that without it, God's presence cannot be fully enjoyed.

James 4:8 exhorts us to draw near to God by (figuratively) washing our hands and purifying our hearts so that He can come near to us in return.

After God delivered His people in Egypt and led them out to where He wanted them to first experience His presence at Mt. Sinai, He gave them specific instructions to purify themselves for three days so that they would be ready for Him to manifest His presence (Exodus

19:10-11). Centuries later in remembrance of purity as a prerequisite for the manifestation of God's presence, after Israel had slipped into idolatry and later repented for their ways under King Hezekiah, Hezekiah ordered the temple to be completely purified before it was rededicated to the Lord and reopened as a house of worship (2 Chronicles 29:18). In both instances, God responded favorably to the invitation of His presence by purity, manifesting Himself on Mt. Sinai with a powerful, tangible introduction of Himself to His people, and in Hezekiah's day with blessings and provision throughout Hezekiah's reign as well as divine protection against the Assyrians, one of the most evil armies to have ever existed.

> "You are to be a pure container of Christ."
> 2 Timothy 2:21 TPT

God is attracted to purity. The atmosphere of heaven is holy and so to Him, purity feels like home. This is why God instructed the Israelites at Mt. Sinai to purify themselves in preparation to receive His presence—He wanted to be at home with His people, and He knew the surest way to prepare a home for Himself among His people would be to invite His people to purity.

Purity creates a resting place for God's presence, a home for the Almighty to make a dwelling on earth. The significance of this cannot be overstated because to invite the Lord is to invite the very source of all power and authority to take up residence on earth. When God takes up residence in a person or place, the impossible becomes possible; nothing is beyond limits.

In addition to inviting His very presence, purity also has a way of qualifying us to be entrusted with the deep things of God's heart. Purity is the quality that enables one person to open up his or her heart to another. People generally only entrust the deepest parts of their hearts to those they perceive as having pure motives, those who can be trusted to hold those deep things responsibly and confidentially, and in so doing, can help bear one another's burdens without any thought of using the information they receive for selfish gain.

It is the same way with God. Trust must always be won; it is never an assumption or a right. God shares the deep things of His heart with those who have won His trust—those He calls His friends.

"Shall I hide from Abraham what I am about to do?" God asked in Genesis 18:17. The implied answer was, "Of course not!" God shares His heart with His friends just like we do, and God considered Abraham His friend (Isaiah 41:8, James 2:23).

Jesus said something similar about the way He reveals the deep mysteries of the Father to those He considers His friends. "No longer do I call you servants," Jesus said to those who had won His trust, "for the servant does not know what his master is doing; but I have called you friends, for all that I have heard from my Father I have made known to you" (John 15:15).

God's heart doesn't change; He is the same yesterday, today, and forever. He always has and always will share the deepest parts of Himself with those He calls His friends, and the quality He is looking for in His friends is purity. Jesus said in Mathew 5:8 (NLT), "God blesses those whose hearts are pure, for they will see God." Purity gives us eyes to see the secrets and desires of God's heart. What an honor and a privilege that is.

He will always share the deepest parts of Himself with those He calls His friends, and the quality He is looking for in His friends is purity.

Endowed with divine wisdom, King Solomon considered the purity that invites God's presence and wins God's trust to be the most desirable and defining characteristic of a godly woman: "Who can find a virtuous woman?" he asks, "for her price is far above rubies" (Proverbs 31:10 KJV). I love that aspect of my calling and identity as a woman. Purity enables us to carry God's heart in a way nothing else can, and to me, there is no higher calling and no greater gift than for God Himself to entrust His heart to me.

Aligning our Strength

In addition to inviting God's presence, purity also realigns motives. Without purity, strength tends to abuse. To abuse something is to use it in a way that is not in accordance with its intended purpose. Purity keeps our strength aligned with divine purpose. It acts as the guardrails for the road, the banks for the river. Without sturdy banks, the strength of a river can sweep away and destroy everything in its path, but with proper steering by the riverbank, those same waters carry life-giving sustenance and beauty, enabling life in all its forms to flourish. Purity is the riverbank that allows our strength as women to remain in Godly alignment and to be directed toward the life-giving purposes God intended.

> **Grace is the empowerment to go beyond human ability.**

God in His grace gives us ability to do (and *be*) far more than our human capacity allows. The very definition of grace is the empowerment to go beyond human ability. Grace infuses "super" into our "natural" in order to manifest the *supernatural*. We are not able to obtain salvation by human means, but grace empowers a supernatural transaction that enables us to be saved. Similarly, we are not able to walk out our faith or fulfill any part of our callings and destinies in our own strength; we need God's grace to empower us. "Are you so foolish?" Paul asked the Galatian church, "Having begun by the Spirit, are you now being perfected by the flesh?" (Galatians 3:3). These were some of Paul's most passionate words recorded in a letter to a church. He was appalled at the abandonment of grace, yet we do this all the time!

It is our human nature to think we can do this life on our own. When we see someone operating at a high level of gifting or walking out an impressive calling, we can tend to assume that gifts and callings are rewards for the super-spiritual. However, this is simply not true. The word for "gift" in the Greek comes from the same root word as the Greek word for "grace". Gifts are specific manifestations of grace.

They are in essence packaged up bundles of grace that find expression in a form that we can identify as a particular "gift".

God's grace is therefore what empowers every part of our journey, starting with salvation and continuing on all our lives. Romans 11:29 says that the gifts and calling of God are irrevocable. God gives gifts and callings out of His goodness, and He doesn't take them back, even when we fail to steward them well—even when we have fallen into sin—because gifting and calling are not dependent on human performance.

Purity is fundamental to the accomplishment of God's purposes on earth.

Because it is truly all by grace, and because our gifts and callings are given irrevocably and never retracted regardless of what we do with them, it is possible for us to abuse our gifts and callings. We can choose to use our God-given gifts, talents, and abilities for selfish gain, building our own kingdoms instead of God's Kingdom. We therefore need purity of heart to direct our gifting and callings to the fulfillment of divine purposes. The more giftedness or the greater the calling God places on our lives, the more important it is to remain in the place of purity that invites His presence and directs His power toward His purpose.

> "Her shining light will not be extinguished, no matter how dark the night."
>
> Proverbs 31:18 TPT

The purity of woman was designed to motivate leaders to pursue righteousness and justice and to ground the Church in the beauty of God's holiness. God's irrevocable gifts and callings serve no lasting Kingdom purpose if not directed by purity, and therefore purity is fundamental to the accomplishment of God's purposes on earth. When purity is properly recognized for what it is, it has a way of aligning earth's efforts with heaven's vision, guiding the force of the river through the edges of the riverbank so it can reach its intended destiny.

Purity is Protective

Purity is also an incredibly important covering for life and ministry. Purity of heart is protective against the Enemy's devices to manipulate human interactions for the Enemy's purposes. Life is about relationships. First and foremost, it is about our relationship with God, and then it is about loving the people around us with His love until they come into the image of Christ and step into the fullness of their unique callings and destinies.

Purity is a fundamental prerequisite to relationship the way God intended. First, it is fundamentally required for proper relationship with Him, and second, it is required for safe and meaningful relationship with another human in any capacity. When our relationships start from the foundation of purity, it is infinitely more difficult for the Enemy to infiltrate those relationships because purity is birthed out of complete surrender to King Jesus, and human connection that is founded on connection with Him is ultimately indestructible, despite whatever setbacks we encounter from the Enemy onslaught.

While the foundation of purity is incredibly protective, it is not a guarantee we won't fall. Humans are imperfect, and this side of heaven, our communications and interactions with other humans will not be completely immune to the Enemy's devices. But even so, purity is ultimately protective of the relationship, keeping it from being irrevocably lost. Purity of heart enables restoration after a fall or a falling out. It enables renewed trust and restored relationship at a rate not possible without purity of heart.

Purity of heart is also protective against false accusation and slander. Whatever others might think, say, or do out of jealousy or insecurity, purity enables those untruths and half-truths to slip off, unable to stick with us or make an impact.

I recently saw the protective aspect of purity played out in my own life when I was falsely accused by a prominent leader in my church. Friends who know me well were as shocked as I had been that something so discordant with my character could be posited. As much as it hurt, I knew that resorting to a posture of self-defense would only serve to validate the assumptions about my character, and that the only way to redeem the situation would be to keep my thoughts and motives toward this person pure, allowing my purity of heart to serve as my unspoken defense while waiting on God to illuminate truth in His way and His timing. I reminded my heart that people are not my enemy and that instead of bitterness or anger, this person needed my prayers for freedom from the lies she was believing.

> **I reminded my heart that people are not my enemy.**

Not long after, another leader whom I had assumed believed the things spoken about me publicly praised me and thanked me for my leadership in the church. I was truly so surprised! But I knew that by choosing to keep my heart pure and praying for the person who had falsely accused me instead of allowing myself to dwell in the hurt, I made room for God to quickly start revealing the truth, restore me, and raise me up in the eyes of these leaders to a place of honor that was even beyond what I'd had before.

In thinking of this in allegorical form, I picture a pure gold surface next to a surface of unrefined gold with little bits of sand and debris scattered throughout. If you were to throw some dirt all over both surfaces, the unrefined one would be much harder to clean, because those little pieces of sand would hang on to the dirt. Similarly, dirt sticks more easily in our lives when there are pieces of sand stuck in our gold! When our lives and hearts are purified, there is nothing for the dirt to hang on to and so those false accusations and assumptions slide off of us into forgotten oblivion much more easily.

Running after Purity

After we have received the righteousness of Jesus through saving faith in His death and resurrection, what happens if we compromise the purity He won for us and allow our hearts to be filled with something other than Him? James 4:8 (NLT) instructs us to "purify [our] hearts" when our "loyalty is divided between God and the world." But how do we recapture the singleness of heart that defines purity?

Jumping back into my own story, after my fall into sin I never imagined myself capable of, I knew the only proper response was repentance. To repent means literally to "turn around," to stop what you are doing and the direction you are headed and to instead go in the opposite direction. It took me much longer to fully separate myself from temptation than I'd like to admit. Part of me was chasing after Jesus but another part of me was chasing validation from the other person, and so my heart was divided.

Step one in purifying my heart involved truly and definitively separating myself from the pursuit of this person's validation, taking myself away from the alternate "substance" (human validation) with which I was trying to fill myself up so that I could be purified by being filled with one substance alone (Jesus).

The process of purifying ourselves really comes down to this: the fear of the Lord. To fear the Lord does not mean to be afraid of Him, but is in essence to place His opinion above all other opinions. The fear of the Lord is in opposition to the fear of man—at any given time, we are all either fearing the Lord or we are fearing man. To fear man is to value a certain person's opinion or a group's opinion above all other opinions, whereas to fear the Lord is to reverence Him and respect Him in such a way that we value His opinion more than that of any human.

> **To fear the Lord does not mean to be afraid of Him, but is in essence to place His opinion above all other opinions.**

Put another way, to fear the Lord is to give Him our continuous and irrevocable yes—the kind of yes captured by Job's statement: "Though He slay me, yet will I trust Him" (Job 13:15 NKJV). It's the kind of yes that says, "Not my will, but yours be done" (Luke 22:42), the kind that puts me second, and God first, the kind that keeps on saying yes to Him, no matter how hard it gets or how high the cost, the kind that *says yes before the question is even asked* because the question doesn't even matter—whatever God asks, my answer is "yes". That is what it is to fear the Lord. To fear the Lord is to maintain the heart of purity that enables the divine presence, protection, and purpose God's daughters were designed to release.

> "...*this virtuous woman lives in the wonder, awe, and fear of the Lord. She will be praised throughout eternity.*"
>
> Proverbs 31:30 TPT

There is nothing God can't do with our "yes". Our "yes" is all He needs; it is all He is waiting on. Our "yes" takes off all earthly boundaries and limitations, making the impossible possible and the unseen seen. 2 Corinthians 1:20 says that "all the promises of God find their Yes in him. That is why it is through him that we utter our Amen to God for his glory." The word "Amen" conveys the idea of "so be it" or "let it be done". In other words, "yes". Our promises are already "yes" in Jesus—they are just waiting on us to come into agreement with Him so they can be released on earth for His glory.

After surrendering my contaminating substance and choosing the fear of the Lord over the validation of man, step two in my restoration process was even harder for me—I had to accept the free gift of redemption! I kept asking the Lord to forgive me and wash me clean, but I was wallowing in condemnation too much to believe that He did indeed forgive and restore me. God was showing me that I needed healing, yet I kept thinking this was something *I* needed to do, while all the while He was asking me to let *Him* be my Healer.

This went on for months until one day I completely lost my temper with the Lord. "I know I need healing but I don't know what I need to do to be healed!" I shouted. I had apologized to everyone I had hurt and asked for the Lord's forgiveness and separated myself from the temptation. Still I was consumed by regret and shame. My perfectionism had led to the bondage of people-pleasing that in turn led to compromise. Now my pride was keeping me in a cycle of performance, and the need to prove myself worthy was preventing me from receiving the grace He wanted to give. In a dramatic outburst, I told the Lord that He shouldn't have grace for me, that I wasn't worthy, and that He should give up on me.

> **My perfectionism had led to the bondage of people-pleasing that in turn led to compromise.**

I held firmly to this position that entire night. Then the next morning while sitting quietly with the Lord, He started telling me about all the wonderful things that were in His heart for me. "Umm, what?" I questioned. "Are you ignoring the fact I just spent all this time yelling at you, angry at my inability to prove myself and frustrated that I can't earn your grace?" "Yes," I could feel His amused smile behind the response, "That is the point. That is grace." He reminded me that there is literally nothing I could come up with that can surprise Him. He already knows the deepest darkness I'm capable of, and still His grace is stronger. Redemption is stronger.

That day, I surrendered to grace in a way I had never been able to before. I finally understood and actually chose to believe in the power of redemption. Since then, I have experienced the sweet freedom of Jesus that truly compares to nothing else on earth. No more proving, no more striving. My perfectionism is swallowed up in victory, forever laid to rest at the foot of the cross.

God is a Gentleman. He won't force His way into places He is not invited. But when we say yes, He comes in with power and love to "achieve infinitely more than your greatest request, your most unbelievable dream, and exceed your wildest imagination! He will outdo them all" (Ephesians 3:20 TPT).

The fear of the Lord opens doors that cannot be opened in any other way. With those doors flung wide, Jesus comes in to do what only He can do, and the watching world stands amazed as He and His love accomplish great things through us. That is the power of purity. Purity makes us vessels to house His manifest presence, and when God shows up in such a tangible way in our lives, there is nothing He can't do through us.

> *"Her lamp does not go out, but it burns continually through the night [she is prepared for whatever lies ahead]."*
> Proverbs 31:18 AMP

Prayer

Partnering with God

Prayer is not something I always knew how to do or even particularly wanted to do. I had so many misperceptions about what prayer is and for so long saw it more as a duty than a privilege. My life was forever changed when I became friends with people who have a deep love for prayer and truly appreciate the privilege and honor prayer is! I think prayer is something that is best taught by example. Seeing the way Jesus prayed and the way His lifestyle of prayer empowered His life and ministry is what stirred up in the disciples a desire to understand and participate in prayer themselves and when they made the request, "Lord, teach us to pray," (Luke 11:1 NKJV), Jesus responded by giving them an example prayer (Luke 11:2-4). Similarly, for me it was seeing the lifestyle of prayer in my friends that stirred in me a desire to experience the kind of prayer life they exhibited, and it was watching them pray that served as my most effective teacher.

Prayer is now my absolute favorite part of my day, and most mornings the Lord has to at some point tell me to stop sitting with Him and go get ready for work so I won't be late! The Lord is my favorite person to talk with and spend time with, and while I especially love the dedicated, undistracted time with Him, I also love being able to talk and commune with Him throughout my whole day. Prayer is both a lifestyle and an appointment, the 24/7 phone line and the dedicated phone call, the walking with God and the carving out time for Him.

> **Prayer is both a lifestyle and an appointment, the 24/7 phone line and the dedicated phone call.**

Prayer is essentially communion with God. It is getting to know His heart, His dreams, His visions, His hurts, His desires. It is also learning what He sees in us—our desires, our gifting and callings, our identity, and our relationship with Him. It is coming to the place of partnering with God, both for everyday life and for the mighty things He wants to release through us.

Women of divine power and purpose must first and foremost be women of prayer. Prayer is the fuel in our tank, the weapon in our arsenal, and the anchor for our hearts. Prayer is also the reason for every power we manifest and every purpose we fulfill because communion with our Maker is the very essence of what life is about. It is the heartbeat of life because it is the process for the very things we were created for—fellowship and partnership with God.

The Secret Place

Prayer can happen at any moment and every moment; it is a state of being in constant communication with the Lord and a constant state of listening for Him to speak. 1 Thessalonians 5:17 says to "pray without ceasing." I love that we can train our spirits to be in constant communion with the Holy Spirit, praying continually throughout our day. Proverbs 31:18 (AMP) says of the woman who fears the Lord,

"Her lamp does not go out, but it burns continually through the night." The language of this verse reminds me of the parable Jesus told in which five of ten virgins were wise to take extra oil in order to keep their lamps burning until the bridegroom (Jesus) arrived (see Matthew 25). Oil in Scripture is often symbolic of the Holy Spirit and it is the Holy Spirit in us that makes us light to the world (Matthew 5:14-16). We let our light shine by allowing the Holy Spirit to have free rein in us, which requires communion with Him through prayer.

Being in constant communion with the Lord is the way life was meant to be lived. At the same time, a lifestyle of continual prayer is best cultivated in dedicated time alone with the Lord because prayer is strongest and deepest in the secret place. Jesus was known to often get away by Himself to pray (Luke 5:16) and He instructed His disciples to do the same: "When you pray, go into your room and shut the door and pray to your Father who is in secret. And your Father who sees in secret will reward you" (Matthew 6:6).

A lifestyle of continual prayer is best cultivated in dedicated time alone with the Lord.

In our one-on-one time with the Lord, we get to know Him in a way that is incomparable. Just as getting to know a person requires observing their interactions with others as well as hearing his or her heart in uninterrupted and undistracted one-on-one time, so it is with the Lord.

God is indeed omnipresent, able to be everywhere at once, but He reserves a special outpouring of Himself—a unique manifestation of His presence—for those who will seek Him in the secret place. Jesus promised a reward from the Father for those who meet Him there, and there is no greater reward than to know Him, to be trusted with His heart, and to be invited to be His friend.

So much could be said about prayer in the secret place. The types of communication we can have with the Lord are even more numerous than the types of communication we can have with people because His resources and ingenuity are limitless. When the disciples asked Jesus to teach them to pray, His example prayer demonstrated various types of interactions with God including worship, affirmation of relationship and identity, declaration of God's purposes, petition for provision, repentance, and spiritual warfare (Matthew 6:9-13). Any one of these types of prayer can be the focus of dedicated hours of communion with the Lord and each one could have volumes of books written about it. For our purposes here though, there are three particular aspects of prayer in the secret place that I think are so important for releasing our God-given power and purpose as women created in His image: intimacy, preparation, and petition.

The Place of Intimacy

The secret place is first and foremost the place of intimacy. Before mountain-moving, giant-slaying, or stronghold-destroying (and don't get me wrong, prayer is for all those things!), prayer is first and foremost about intimacy with our Maker.

God tasked us with exercising dominion over the earth (Genesis 1:26-28) and advancing His Kingdom for His glory (Luke 17:21). But before He will release us to accomplish these assignments, His most important priority is to bring us into relationship with Himself and ensure our understanding of our identity as His daughters. Throughout history, it has been those who have known the most intimacy with the Lord who have accomplished the most for His Kingdom. Intimacy with the Lord brings us to know our Creator and ourselves in a way nothing else can, and there is no greater driver of destiny than to know one's identity and to be both fully known and fully loved by another.

> **It is those who have known the most intimacy with the Lord that have accomplished the most for His Kingdom.**

For me, intimacy with the Lord looks different from day to day. In many ways, to commune with the Lord is simply to just *be with* Him. Every meeting with Jesus is different, unique to the season and circumstances and to the things that are on His heart and mine. Some days, I have a lot to say and He does more of the listening as I pour out my heart, whether it be grief and lament, anger and frustration, worship and adoration, or the sorrow of repentance.

Other days I don't have much to say, but He does. I love those days. On those occasions, I get out my journal and start writing out what He is speaking. Sometimes He speaks faster than I can write and it is hard to keep up! And sometimes I have to interrupt Him and ask Him to pause because the things He has in His heart for me are so beautiful that I have to stop and cry before I'm ready for Him to continue.

Then there are days in which neither of us have much to say, and we are content to simply be in each other's company. There is something indescribable and irreplaceable about those times with Him. In those moments when the Lord tells me He has no agenda other than to just be with me, something in me shifts so that the whole way I look at life is different. My performance-driven, acceptance-seeking efforts suddenly become inconsequential, and my insecurities stemming from my incorrect assumptions about the Lord's expectations and demands instantly dissipate.

> **When the Lord tells me He has no agenda other than to just be with me, something in me shifts.**

I am reminded of a pair of sisters Jesus went to visit in a town called Bethany. Martha was excited to see Jesus. She had a gift of hospitality and she was so excited to manifest her gift. She eagerly welcomed Jesus into her house and poured herself into serving Him. Throughout the evening though, something shifted in Martha. What began as an act of love became an act of performance. She was no longer serving Jesus because she wanted to, but because she felt she had to in order to prove herself worthy of His acceptance. Martha became jealous of her sister

Mary, who had freely accepted Jesus' love and was therefore released to simply be with Him, while Martha felt that she had to prove herself to earn His love. In frustrated jealousy of Mary's freedom, Martha finally pointed out Mary's lack of frenzy-assistance and rebuked her sister in front of the entire dinner party. Jesus lovingly countered this rebuke, pointing out that Martha had allowed herself to become distracted from what was most important and that Mary had done the one thing that was necessary (Luke 10:42).

Intimacy with Jesus gives meaning to every other relationship, every gift and calling, and every endeavor to advance His Kingdom. Martha had gifts and callings to manifest in her life, but she had yet to ground them in a love relationship with Jesus and therefore they did not bring the fulfillment she was hoping for. Just as the Proverbs 31 woman kept her lamps burning (v18), Mary kept the lamp of God's Spirit burning inside her through continual communion with her Lord. Martha on the other hand, was not communing with the source of light and life and therefore her lamp was burning low, giving way to frustration and jealousy. Martha was using her gifts in an attempt to *prove* her identity rather than letting her gifts flow from her identity. Martha, like all of us, needed time in the secret place with her Creator. She needed to learn about His heart for her before she could be released to properly carry out her gifts and callings.

The Place of Preparation

Preparation is about knowing who I am, who my team is, and what resources are available to me. The secret place is the place of preparation because prayer is where I come to know my identity, receive my assignments, align my heart with His, and see fear driven out by His perfect love. Proverbs 31:18 in the Amplified Bible says of the woman walking out her God-given calling, "Her lamp does not go out, but it burns continually through the night [she is prepared for whatever lies ahead]." Communing with God in the secret place prepares us for anything life brings our way because as the one who holds our future in His hands, God is our perfect source of stability, strength, and direction.

Of the many aspects of preparation that take place in the secret place, identity is by far the most foundational and necessary prerequisite for the release of a move of God. It is there that I come to know who I am apart from preconceived ideas, labels that have been placed on me, and perceptions of people who look only at outward evidence rather than inward design. It is also where I meet one-on-one with my Designer, who knows exactly what He placed within me, what He designed me to do, and how the Enemy has strategically covered up the most powerful parts of me that God still sees, even if I don't.

> **Identity is by far the most foundational prerequisite for the release of a move of God.**

The preparation process is not always easy. Identity-revealing involves the removal of false sources of identity, and separation from sources of validation other than God. This process is often painful because to be stripped of false identity leaves us (temporarily) in a place of uncertainty about who we are and what the future holds.

In the Bible we catch a glimpse of the preparation process in the life of Queen Esther. She was a woman who lived out her call as a "woman of valor", and yet I can't help but notice the long backstory, the years of behind-the-scenes preparation that formed Esther into the woman she needed to be to confidently step into the calling on her life. The Bible introduces us to Esther shortly after the king of Persia dismissed Queen Vashti for failing to present herself at his banquet party and subsequently accepted the advice to search the land for beautiful women to add to his harem. The plan was that he would select a new queen from among these women. In execution of this plan, Esther (whose original Hebrew name was Hadassah) was taken to the king's palace and forced to undergo a twelve-month purification process before being introduced to the king. Besides the fact that the process itself was humiliating and uncomfortable, Esther was also affected by the emotional turmoil of being separated from her people, her culture, her religion, her only living family member—in short, everything she had defined herself by. Esther had twelve months in which to complete the transformation from Jewish orphan to Persian queen. I am sure that throughout the preparation process there were many sleepless nights, prayers of desperation, and tears of devastation, but that pain of stripping away her past identity is what positioned Esther (spoiler alert!) to fulfill her God-given call to deliver and govern her people.

There comes a moment in every woman's life when she needs to choose to receive her validation from the only source worthy of defining her. Security, pleasure, status or power, and the approval of a certain person or people are not necessarily wrong in and of themselves, but they can easily transform into idols in our lives when they take the place of God as our source of identity.

In the secret place, He refines and defines. He releases new dimensions and new layers that have been covered by fear and pretense to reveal the daughter who has been hiding underneath. In my personal journey, allowing the Lord to show me my true identity has been a long process because acceptance by people has been a longstanding idol in my life and it can be so hard for me to truly separate my identity from those whose approval I just can't imagine living without.

> **There comes a moment in every woman's life when she needs to choose to receive her validation from the only source worthy of defining her.**

My testimony largely consists of a process of allowing the Lord to strip me of false sources of identity—like friendships. The first time I faced this battle was in high school where I ended up in a situation in which I had to choose between standing up for what was right, or doing the popular thing and covering up a crime. Standing in the gap for what was right cost me my closest friendships and left me with a lot of 'friendship insecurity' as I started college, but it also left room for God to take His rightful place as my closest friend, sparking the beginning of an intimacy with Him that I've never regretted.

The Lord and I proceeded to go through a similar process in various areas of my life over many years—I would ask Him to strip me of a false source of identity and He would do so, then I would take some time to recover (some were harder than others!) but eventually agree with Him that being free of that thing's control over my life was worth it and therefore would ask Him to do it again in whatever area of my life He wanted to address next, and the cycle would start over! We went through so many sources of false identity—friendships, grades, achievements, romantic relationships, family, bosses, authority figures, and spiritual leaders to name a few. Finding true identity requires separation, but that cost is more than worth the prize of freedom. The Lord has so many things to speak over us about who we are and who He sees us to be if we would only allow our hearts to go through the hard work of separation from alternative definers so that the Lord can be the one and only one we allow to define us.

Finding our true identity requires separation.

The first part of preparation is knowing ourselves—our true identities. The second part is coming to know the Lord's heart so we can perceive what it is He wants to release through us, and how we can do that. In Isaiah 55:8-9 the Lord tells us, "My thoughts are not your thoughts, neither are your ways my ways... For as the heavens are higher than the earth, so are my ways higher than your ways and my thoughts than your thoughts." The highest level of problem-solving the human mind is capable of does not even come close to comparing to the strategies, creativity, and solutions available in the mind and heart of God.

God honors the free will He gave to mankind and He generally will not step in unless we invite Him to. Only in very extreme circumstances at monumental moments in history has God stepped in to override mankind's will. Prayer is so important because it is the avenue through which the Lord chooses to release the things He wants to release on the earth. Prayer is where our problems meet divine strategies and where earthly roadblocks meet heavenly breakthroughs. However, to invite Him to do what He wants to do, we first must know what it is He wants to do.

Beyond even the amazing privilege of discovering divine strategies and solutions, the secret place is also where we are given access to the Lord's heart and desires. Romans 8:26 (NLT) says, "We don't know what God wants us to pray for, but the Holy Spirit prays for us with groanings that cannot be expressed in words." Since the Holy Spirit knows the deepest secrets of God's heart (1 Corinthians 2:10-11), we can ask the Holy Spirit what is in God's heart and what He wants to release through us so that we are prepared to pray the powerful prayers that release the hand of God into our world.

The Place of Petition

Prayer is where the battle takes place. Living in the physical world with physical bodies and physical manifestations of our problems, we can tend to look to the physical world for evidence of victory. However, the Bible says that our struggle is "not against flesh and blood, but against the rulers, against the authorities, against the cosmic powers over this present darkness, against the spiritual forces of evil in the heavenly places" (Ephesians 6:12). In other words, the real battle is not physical. People are not the enemy; the Enemy (the devil) is the enemy!

Prayer is where the battle takes place.

Because the battle is not in the physical realm, the evidence of victory is also not in the physical. Hebrews 11:1 says that faith is the evidence of what is not yet seen. So, the battle is unseen and the evidence of impending victory (faith) is also unseen. It is an entirely spiritual transaction. We identify demonic strategies and the appropriate retaliation through spiritual discernment, then declare God's truth and send out angel armies in the spirit, and finally, we watch for the impact of our warfare in the spirit as well, monitoring the effectiveness of our strategies and our progress toward victory through the unseen evidence of faith.

As we check our progress and impact, we have to remind ourselves that evidence is not seen in the change of a physical situation, but rather perceived in the presence of faith. The amazing thing about letting faith be our unseen evidence is that faith circles back to strengthen the process itself, giving us the fuel to continue praying those effective, faith-evidence-producing prayers. Faith breeds evidence, which empowers effective prayer, which then produces more evidence, and so on. Faith is therefore the energy fueling effective prayer!

Faith is the energy that fuels effective prayer.

God responds to faith. Countless times in everyday interactions when people would experience the healing power of God, Jesus would explain that it was their faith that made them well. God has all these amazing things in His heart for us, but they cannot be released without our faith.

Because of the power faith carries to unlock blessing, lack of faith (or more accurately, faith in people or things other than God) also devastates the Lord in a way quite unlike anything else. Both Matthew and Mark observed that Jesus' miracles were hindered in His hometown due to the unbelief of the people there (Matthew 13:58, Mark 6:5) and some of Jesus' most agonizing words were a lament over the city of Jerusalem for refusing to trust the love and protection He had longed to give (Matthew 23:37).

God does not force us to accept His blessings, and since faith is the spiritual equivalent of telling the Lord we accept what He wants to give, there are many things He won't give us without that accepting "yes" of faith. Faith stirs heaven to action, and women of faith-filled prayer have unrivaled power to release the desires that are in the Father's heart. As we seek to know and release His heart, we discover something I think is remarkable—that the Father has a special place in His heart for His daughters when we come to Him with those heartfelt, agonizing prayers of mountain-moving, God-activating faith.

> **Faith stirs heaven to action, and women of faith-filled prayer have unrivaled power to release the desires that are in the Father's heart.**

One woman who demonstrated well the power of a faith-filled woman contending for the things God had in His heart for her was Hannah. She was a woman who persevered in prayer despite incurring ridicule from peers and the scorn of a society that had no patience to wait on her miracle.

We meet Hannah at the very beginning of 1 Samuel, during a time of transition in Israel's history. The time of governance by local judges was coming to an end, as the people were getting restless with their current system and anxious to assimilate their governing structure to reflect those of the surrounding nations. Hannah did not know about the historical shifts on the horizon of her nation's future but God did, and He saw something in Hannah that led Him to invite her into His overarching redemption plan for His people.

Hannah was the favored of two wives of a man named Elkanah, and the deep burden she carried was that she was unable to have children. Every year, Elkanah would go to Shiloh to worship and sacrifice to the Lord, and every year Hannah would go with him to beg the Lord to give her a child. Meanwhile, Elkanah's other wife, Peninnah, would mock Hannah for her continued barren state. "God doesn't hear your prayers," I imagine Peninnah taunting, "Why bother?"

However, rather than discourage Hannah into giving up hope,

Peninnah's taunts drove Hannah deeper into heartfelt prayer. "Her lamp [did] not go out" (Proverbs 31:18) as she "continue[d] steadfastly in prayer" (Colossians 4:2). This was no half-hearted, lip-service prayer. It was a prayer of desperation, a prayer of agony, a prayer that required mustering up everything in her being to even formulate coherent thoughts to present to the Lord. "She was deeply distressed and prayed to the Lord and wept bitterly," 1 Samuel 1:10 says.

Hannah was so distressed that when Eli the priest noticed her, he assumed she was drunk! Hannah protested this assumption and explained, "I have been pouring out my soul before the Lord… I have been speaking out of my great anxiety and vexation" (1 Samuel 1:15-16).

Pouring out your soul in deep distress, bitter tears, and vexation. Have you ever prayed like that? Let me tell you, desperation is a powerful driving force; it can either drive us to seek answers in other places, or it can drive us deep into the heart of the Father. Hannah chose the latter. She recognized she had no power of her own to change her circumstances, and in that place, she chose to lay everything at the feet of her Creator.

Desperation is a powerful driving force.

Desperation, when properly directed, can be a powerful activator of faith. We don't have to wait for that place of desperation before activating our faith, but oftentimes it is only as we get to the end of our self-sufficiency that we finally give God permission to do what He wants to do.

Hannah was in just such a state when Eli found her, and once his initial assumptions were corrected, Eli recognized that place of desperation. More importantly, he recognized the faith she had channeled her desperation into activating. Eli knew that God responds to faith, and so upon recognizing her faith, he called out the promise as good as done. "Go in peace and the God of Israel grant your petition that you have made to him," he said to her (1 Samuel 1:17).

Hannah truly was a woman of faith. Even though she had no physical evidence of her healing, and Peninnah was still mocking, and nothing felt different about her situation, Hannah believed Eli so deeply that she was no longer even sad (1 Samuel 1:18). Her whole demeanor changed because, in her mind, her prayer was already answered in the spiritual realm even though she didn't yet have the evidence of it in the physical.

Hannah went on to miraculously conceive and give birth to a son, Samuel, who later became the prophet who anointed King David, a forerunner and important ancestor of Jesus. Hannah had a critical role in God's redemptive plan for Israel, paving the way for King David's destiny and ultimately to the line that would birth the Messiah. It was her faith that released the destiny God had in His heart for her, her family, her nation, and ultimately the world.

Hannah's faith was marked by her persistence. She knew the Father's heart well enough to know that the desire in her heart for a child was one that He had placed within her, and therefore she was not going to stop contending for her miracle.

God responds to both faith and persistence, and there is a fundamental connection between the two. Jesus once told His disciples a parable that was specifically aimed at demonstrating the importance of persistence in prayer. In this particular parable, a widow repeatedly approaches a local judge to ask for justice in a situation in which she had been wronged. She is so persistent that the judge eventually agrees to bring justice for her, even though he is an immoral man who otherwise would not have risen up to fight for her. After finishing the story, Jesus comments, "Will not God give justice to his elect, who cry to him day and night?... I tell you, he will give justice to them speedily. Nevertheless, when the Son of Man comes, will he find faith on the earth?" (Luke 18:7-8).

Isn't it interesting that it is the widow's persistence that is equated to faith? The passage opens with the comment that this story was meant to encourage Jesus' followers to pray persistently without giving up (Luke 18:1) and concludes with a warning that the move of God cannot be activated without faith.

I think persistence does two things. First, it brings us to the place of faith, because as humans we so often have to contend for things persistently before we finally reach the end of our self-sufficiency and are willing to truly believe that unless God does it, there is no other way for our miracle to happen. It is from that place of wholehearted dependence on the Lord that we are ready to enter the realm of faith. Faith moves the hand of God, and persistence is often the facilitator we need to reach the place of God-activating faith in our hearts.

The other thing persistence does is prove our faith—not to God, but to ourselves. God has given us each a sufficient measure of faith (Romans 12:3) for everything He has called us to, but we ourselves often don't know how much faith we are capable of stepping into unless God brings us to the outer limits of that faith.

Hebrews 11:13 says that the men and women who have gone before us to leave a legacy of faith did not need physical evidence, and were content to "greet [their promises] afar off." I love the simplicity of that statement. They were content to warmly welcome their promises, even though there were no signs of their impending fulfillment in the natural. They knew that battles are won in the spirit before they manifest in the physical, and they were content to live in that place of *spiritual* fulfillment.

Like Jesus' hometown experienced, unbelief (i.e., faith in people or things other than God) is the surest way to hinder a move of God. On the other hand, faith in the Almighty releases power that makes the impossible possible, the unseen seen, and dead things alive. There is nothing God can't do with our "yes" of faith. God didn't shortchange anyone in their faith allotment; we already have all the faith we need for our journey. All that is up to us is to put our faith into action through alignment with the Father's heart, proclaiming into the physical what God sees in the spiritual so He can release the things that are in His heart for us.

The secret place is the place of intimacy, preparation, and miracle-releasing. Through prayer, we come to know the Lord, our identities, and the strategies needed for atmosphere-shifting, God-activating, Enemy-defeating prayers and for our active partnership with Him through our gifts and callings.

"Strength and dignity are her clothing and her position is strong and secure; And she smiles at the future [knowing that she and her family are prepared]." Proverbs 31:25 AMP

Peace

The Pace of Abiding

I am a recovering perfectionist. I come from a long line of perfectionists and am not sure what portion of my perfectionism may have come from nature and what portion from nurture but one way or another, perfectionism became a struggle for me at a very young age.

Perfectionism in many ways is the most severe form of people-pleasing. Earning acceptance is a man-made idea rather than a God-made idea (the gospel is all about how we can't earn it and need Jesus!), and when I applied my perfectionist mindset to my view of God, I found myself with a very legalistic and "religious" view of God, feeling a constant need to live up to impossible standards to gain His approval. My self-imposed impossible standards left me with perpetual feelings of unworthiness so I had trouble receiving love and grace. And since it was impossible for me to give what I hadn't first been able to receive, it led me to a place of being overly critical of both myself and others.

Perfectionism is a terrible way to live. It ensnared me in a cycle of perpetual striving to reach impossible standards followed by repeated failure to reach that perfection, followed by shame and condemnation for my lack of perfection which would in turn lead me to respond with higher levels of striving. It was an incredibly stressful way to live! And it is wholly opposed to the gospel of Jesus. Ephesians 2:8-9 (NLT) says, "God saved you by his grace when you believed. And you can't take credit for this; it is a gift from God. Salvation is not a reward for the good things we have done, so none of us can boast about it."

Receiving by grace is much less stressful than attempting to earn something by impossible standards that can never actually be attained! But receiving by grace required the death of my pride and self-sufficiency, and therein lay the heart of the decades-long battle as the Lord slowly chipped away at my hold on perfectionism and wooed my heart to receive His free gift of grace.

Perfectionism is the enemy of peace.

Perfectionism is the enemy of peace. I believe perfectionism is so rampant in our culture and among women in particular, because the Enemy knows that a woman who carries peace wields a destructive weapon against the forces of evil, and he is hard at work to steal our peace.

Identity: The Source of Peace

The reason perfectionism is such an effective peace-stealer is that it misplaces our source of identity. Defining ourselves by our ability to measure up to man-made rules (which is the essence of legalism and religion) is a shaky foundation, first because it largely consists of defining ourselves by the ever-changing opinion of people, and second because there is a tendency to project the opinions of humans onto God, assuming that God must define us the same way people do, which isn't true!

Our inability to meet impossible standards also naturally lends to the defense mechanism of competition, because I can somewhat numb my disappointment in myself for my lack of perfection by finding someone I am "more perfect" than. For us as women, losing our identity to the trap of perfectionism can lead us to competition both with men and (perhaps even more so) with other women, and keeping us contending with each other is an effective strategy the Enemy can use to steal our peace.

The security that comes from knowing who we are is foundational to living in peace. Competition is rooted in the tendency to find our identity and acceptance in people rather than the Lord. More specifically for us as women, I think that striving is often rooted in the subconscious "need" to define ourselves by the approval of men, which leads to competition with each other for that approval. The problem is that people can only look to external things to define us, and so deriving personal validation from people turns our focus from our inner relationship with the Lord toward the external things people define us by.

> **Deriving personal validation from people turns our focus from our inner relationship with the Lord.**

Anything and everything I can come up with to define myself or others by is rooted in the physical world—whether it is appearance or accomplishments or accolades or reputation or status or wealth or recognition from others. All these things we try to define ourselves by are external things, and when it comes to identity, God does not care about any of them. In defining who we are, God cares only about the *internal*—He cares about our hearts.

Daughters of the King, hear this: your identity comes from your heart. It is not your looks, accomplishments, or acknowledgment from that one person whose approval you can't live without. Your identity is only found in your heart, and only God can see into your heart. No human—I don't care how godly or perceptive that person is—can tell you who you are. We *have* to stop going to that person for validation. It doesn't matter if it is your pastor or your husband or the greatest spiritual giant; if that person is human, you have to stop going to him or her for validation. As far as it is possible, intentionally separate yourself from that person's validation for as long as it takes for you to truly start receiving your identity only from the Lord in the secret place. 1 Samuel 16:7 says:

> **No human has the ability or the right to tell me who I am, because no human can see my heart.**

> "The Lord sees not as man sees: man looks on the outward appearance, but the Lord looks on the heart."

God is the only one who can see my heart; therefore, He is the only one who can speak to my identity. No human has the ability or the right to tell me who I am, because no human can see my heart.

I have let people define my identity far more often than I'd like to admit. Whether it was dressing a certain way or carrying myself a certain way or even my career choice and work hours, catering my need for validation to another human's need for validation is ultimately destructive to both parties because it reinforces a false sense of identity for both of us. For example, I've found that if a man needs me to look a certain way to feel good about himself, and I comply with those demands, I am placing both my identity *and* his identity in my appearance. Trust me, that is a lot of pressure on my appearance to carry that much identity, and ultimately it is a very stressful way to live! External things were not designed to carry the weight of my own identity, let alone someone else's, and it isn't healthy for that person any more than it is for me.

We have to determine to not allow these false sources of identity into our hearts, or we risk destroying ourselves as well as the people we are seeking validation from. The Lord longs for us to know beyond doubt that we are His and His alone.

> "But now thus says the Lord, he who created you O Jacob, he who formed you, O Israel: Fear not, for I have redeemed you; I have called you by name, you are mine."
>
> Isaiah 43:1

I encourage you to read this verse over but insert your name in the place of "Jacob", and instead of the name "Israel", ask the Lord what is the new name that He wants to proclaim over you and insert that new name there. Israel was the name the Lord gave Jacob, and He has new names for each of us as well. Revelation 2:17 says that the Lord has a name for each of us and the only ones who know your new name are Him and (after He reveals it to you) you. He creates us and then forms us into the image of our new name; He redeems us and calls us by that new name, and He makes us His.

Daughters, hear the Lord say to you today, "You are *Mine*." You do not belong to any human; even if you feel that human can give you a decent sense of self, it is still only a shadow, and it is not up to the standards of your new name. Jesus sees much more in you than anyone else possibly could see. You belong to no one but Him, and though He redeems us it is up to us to free ourselves from the bondage of human approval. I am reminded of the apostle Paul and Silas being thrown in jail for preaching the gospel as recorded in the book of Acts. An

> "Loose yourself from the bonds of your neck, O captive daughter of Zion." Isaiah 52:2 NKJV

angel came to miraculously unlock their shackles and open prison doors, but it was still up to Paul and Silas to get up and walk out. Similarly, Jesus sets us free yet there is a responsibility on us to get up and walk out of our prison cells!

Daughters of the King, Jesus set you free, so loose yourself! Walk out in freedom, knowing you belong to Him and Him alone. No one else has any rightful claim to you, no matter who it is. When I go to people for validation instead of the Lord, I feel insecure because people and people's opinions are not secure, and that leads to competition in an attempt to preserve fleeting human validation. On the other hand, looking to the Lord for validation leads to a deep, abiding peace through confidence in God's unchanging love and acceptance of His assessment of who I am based on the inward person that no one but He can see. I myself might not even be able to accurately see who I am, but God does. He is my Creator. He hid treasures within my heart and is purifying my heart to bring me into the fullness of my true identity.

In my monumental battle with the Lord over the idea of grace that I mentioned in chapter one, the struggle truly was about identity as I wrestled with the decision to either continue defining myself by my own efforts, or surrender to His definition of me by accepting grace and with courageous humility, deciding to identify myself with this mind-blowingly unattainable (by human standards) person He saw me to be. The lasting peace that accompanies that kind of identity shift is truly indescribable.

Women who live out of this kind of identity rooted in Jesus invite and carry peace in a transformative way. In a world full of constant pressure and unending demands, God equipped women with unique capacity to carry peace by anchoring us in perspective, in priority, and ultimately in His presence.

Anchored in Perspective

Women are equipped to see the big picture. Where men have a more natural ability to hone in on the task at hand and avoid distractions, women have a tendency to think about the interconnectedness of the various aspects of their lives, even when focusing on a particular task.

Woman's natural ability to see the bigger picture is key to her capacity to be a peace carrier because proper perspective is what peace is all about. God's peace is a result of the complete picture that includes

PEACE

not only the earthly viewpoint but also the heavenly viewpoint. The Enemy can easily steal our peace by getting us to focus on one piece of the giant puzzle of life and in so doing cause us to forfeit the viewpoint God sees from.

Proverbs 31:25 (AMP) says that the woman of virtue holds a position that is "strong and secure" and that she "smiles at the future [knowing that she and her family are prepared]". Knowing my loved ones are cared for doesn't come from having given my best human effort to prepare for every possible scenario from an earthly perspective (this breeds fear and anxiety, the opposite of peace!), but from taking on heaven's vantage point and following God's lead, confident in His ability to see beyond the earthly perspective. There is no better preparation and no greater way to usher in the peace that surpasses understanding (Philippians 4:7) than to see from heaven's perspective and follow the instructions of the God who knows everything—including everything that will happen in all my tomorrows. "You will keep in perfect peace all who trust in you, all whose thoughts are fixed on you!" Isaiah says of the Lord (Isaiah 26:3 NLT).

> **Seeing the big picture is a divine trait the Lord equipped woman in a unique way to carry.**

Seeing the big picture is a part of God's nature. It is a divine trait the Lord equipped woman in a unique way to carry. In His infinite wisdom, the Lord knew we as humans would need both the detailed focus and the big-picture perspective to accomplish His purposes, and this balance is one of the many ways He designed men and women to complement each other in our work as Kingdom-builders.

As a people saved by grace through faith in Jesus and given new status as children of God and co-heirs with Christ, the Bible says that God "raised us up with him and seated us with him in the heavenly places in Christ Jesus" (Ephesians 2:6). We therefore see and pray and live not from earth toward heaven, but from heaven toward earth. We have been given access to a new vantage point, and no one can remove us from our heavenly places unless we choose ourselves to give up our heaven seats and live life from a lesser perspective.

Rather than limit our viewpoint, God's peace takes into consideration the truest representation of the circumstances because it looks at what is happening on earth in light of what is happening in heaven. Peace anchors us in heaven's perspective and has power to transcend our limited earthly view, making heaven more real than earth and bringing spiritual realities into their proper place of importance as we look at the world around us. Peace brings earthly perspective into heavenly alignment.

Jesus' mother Mary anchored herself in divine perspective in a remarkable way. I am amazed by her response to receiving news of her supernatural pregnancy. Shortly after being visited by the angel who announced that she would miraculously give birth to the long-awaited Messiah, Mary went to visit her cousin Elizabeth to share the news and praise the Lord:

> "My soul magnifies the Lord, and my spirit rejoices in God my Savior, for he has looked on the humble estate of his servant. For behold, from now on all generations will call me blessed."
>
> Luke 1:46-48

From now on all nations will call her blessed? One day they will. But right now she is unmarried and pregnant and the rumors are starting to spread, questioning her integrity, hurling accusations, and likely blowing things way out of proportion, far beyond what could reasonably be inferred from the facts. Yet Mary anchors herself in divine perspective. This assignment is bigger than her, bigger than her reputation, and by taking heaven's vantage point, Mary has peace. She is "strong and secure" (Proverbs 31:25 AMP) in her identity, in her future, and in her God. She is confident because her sense of self and her validation does not come from the opinion of people, but the acceptance of her King.

Peace imparted by divine viewpoint is a powerful force. When Jesus and His disciples were interrupted by a storm on the sea of Galilee, Jesus was not at all bothered. He had already determined to make His dwelling place in His Father's heart rather than the raging seas of life, and He did not allow the storms to infiltrate His soul. When woken by frantic, soaking-wet disciples, Jesus proclaims peace into the chaos. Notice He does not proclaim confidence, or courage, or strength; He proclaims peace. "Peace! Be still!" He says to the storm (Mark 4:39) and the storm obeys.

Jesus saw the bigger picture. He saw beyond the storm to the heavenly realms that were His true dwelling place, and He knew the storms could not touch His true home. That kind of peace—peace imparted by divine perspective—is powerful. It was the weapon Jesus used to calm that Galilee storm and it is the weapon the Lord imparts to His daughters to wield against the storms of life that thrive in limited, earthly situations.

In my own life, I've seen the power of peace on a practical level in my work. As a critical care doctor, my job in the face of a medical crisis is to be the calmest person in the room. My team is well-trained to respond to emergencies, but when stress and anxiety are high, the tension can prevent us from accessing the knowledge and skills ingrained in us as a team. Peace is so important in those moments, and the peace I carry with me into a medical crisis comes from accessing the heavenly perspective, recognizing that life and death are in the hands of God, and the responsibility for the outcome is His, not mine. Communing with the Holy Spirit about each patient I encounter has given me the assurance that His way is best and that by keeping my heart attuned to Him, I can respond with boldness to proclaim healing into impossible situations or the compassion to comfort grieving families as I follow His lead.

As peace carriers, we are empowered to face the storms head-on.

As peace carriers, we are empowered to face the storms head-on. The Spirit who calmed Mary's heart in the face of shocking news is the same Spirit who calmed raging sea waters, the same Spirit who raised Jesus from the dead, and the same Spirit who is alive in us as God's children and is waiting to be released through the manifestation of peace in a world so desperate for reprieve from the fears of life and the storms of our hearts.

Anchored in Priorities

The second way women impart peace is by being anchored in our priorities—keeping the main thing the main thing. When the cares of this life threaten to drown out the things that are most important, women have a way of redirecting priorities toward people, purpose, and the presence of God.

Our society is increasingly supportive of productivity and promotion at the expense of human beings and relationship. According to society's rules, it is perfectly acceptable and even in many ways expected to work ourselves to death, leaving no time to be with the family we financially support or the people who give our lives meaning. Women are naturally built to recognize the outcast: the unloved, unrecognized, and undervalued people passed by in the hustle of our fast-paced society and forgotten by a culture always looking to get ahead. "She extends her hand to the poor, Yes, she reaches out her hands to the needy," Solomon writes of the woman at rest in her identity as a woman (Proverbs 31:20 NKJV).

Women have a way of redirecting priorities toward people, purpose, and the presence of God.

In the fast-paced, results-oriented, popularity-seeking society we live in, those who we don't see as helpful to the accomplishment of our goals or acceleration of our position can easily slip through the cracks. We can neglect relationships, forgetting that relationship (with others and with the Lord) is what we were created for.

Countless times throughout the gospels, it was noted that Jesus did what He did out of compassion. Whether it was sitting down to teach the multitudes who ran after Him right when He was trying to escape for some much-needed alone time (see Mark 6:31-34), or healing the sick (Matthew 14:14, Matthew 20:34, Mark 1:41), or miraculously multiplying bread and fish to tend to physical needs (Matthew 15:32), or delivering from demons (Mark 5:19), or raising the dead (Luke 7:13), Jesus was often said to have been motivated by compassion. If Jesus' motivation and power came from compassion, then we ought to be running hard after that same compassion power He operated in as well. Women were anointed by God to operate out of that place of compassion by keeping our perspective on the people and relationships in danger of being left behind.

In addition to redirecting our hearts toward people, women are also designed by God to redirect us toward purpose. In the hustle and bustle of life, it is all too easy to get sidetracked building our own kingdoms, forgetting we were given dominion of the earth to build God's Kingdom. God, therefore, designed women to notice when the main thing is no longer the main thing, when the pressure to perform overshadows the reason for performing, and the cares of this life squeeze out our very life. Our Enemy is strategic in his attacks, and if he is unable to stop us from doing good things, he will try to create burnout by piling on *too many* good things so our time is divided and our attention distracted from the God-ordained things.

God designed women to notice when the main thing is no longer the main thing.

Too much of the good-but-not-best drowns out our calling and buries our anointing so deep in our hearts and minds that we no longer even see what they are.

Both men and women were entrusted by God to identify, carry, nurture, guide, and release destiny in the lives of others. This process of identifying and releasing destiny is one of the most important aims of spiritual motherhood and fatherhood, and we as spiritual mothers are healthiest and most adept at carrying out this assignment when we do it in coordination with healthy spiritual fathers. As in the natural world, spiritual mothers release unique aspects of destiny designed to complement, affirm, and accelerate the aspects of destiny released by the fathers.

Spiritual sons and daughters need both mothers and fathers in the faith. We as women are integral to their maturity process. That is why buried destiny drives us so crazy! When we see the main thing buried under piles of the world's demands and expectations, something in us is activated to spring up and strip away the noise, clear out the distractions, and unbury that person's purpose so we can steer it back on track toward its full manifestation.

Ultimately, the way we silence the noise and redirect towards purpose is to lift up the name of Jesus, exalt *His* purposes, and connect us back to His heart. This brings us to the third thing women redirect toward—the presence of God.

> *"Come to me, all who labor and are heavy laden, and I will give you rest."*
>
> Matthew 11:28

People and purpose are important, but when it comes to anchoring us in priorities, nothing compares to the peace imparted by anchoring us in the Lord's presence. The only real priority list by which we live our lives is to be Jesus first, Jesus second, Jesus third. It is all about Jesus. There is nothing and no one else. When we seek first His Kingdom, everything else in life falls seamlessly into place (Matthew 6:33).

Kingdom power anoints the steps of those who live at the pace of peace, the pace of abiding in the presence of God. Our culture celebrates productivity and efficiency and mocks the pace of intimacy with the Lord. But it is in the secret place with Him that we find ourselves, our calling, and our purpose. It is in the secret place that we receive downloads of wise strategies from the Spirit of Counsel, supernatural strength from the Spirit of Might, wisdom and discernment from the Spirit of Wisdom and Understanding, revelation from the Spirit of Knowledge, and renewed perspective from the Spirit of the Fear of the Lord (see Isaiah 11:2). The Lord is our ultimate anchor, grounding us in His love for us, His identity and vision for us, and His callings and futures for us. Living from the place of His presence gives us a "position [that] is strong and secure" so we can, without worry, "smile at the future" (Proverbs 31:25 AMP).

> *"Don't worry about anything; instead, pray about everything. Tell God what you need, and thank him for all he has done. Then you will experience God's peace which exceeds anything we can understand. His peace will guard your hearts and minds as you live in Christ Jesus."*
>
> *Philippians 4:6-7 NLT*

God created woman, in part, so that mankind would not miss life as it passed by, so that we would truly *experience* life and life more abundantly, instead of searching for what we already have. A life lived that way is a life lived in peace through eyes fixated on our one priority, allowing everything else in life to be "added" by Him without effort, just as He promised.

Surrender: The Key to Peace

Peace is not a passive thing. It is not merely the absence of anxiety or striving. As strange as it seems, the Bible tells us we have to work to get to the place of peace. Hebrews 4:9-11 says, "So then, there remains a Sabbath rest for the people of God, for whoever has entered God's rest has also rested from his works as God did from his. Let us therefore strive to enter that rest…"

Strive to enter rest? It sounds like an oxymoron. But the active part is found right in the middle of the passage—we have to actively and intentionally stop our own works. Trying to figure it out by myself and trying to control my situation is a natural human response, and it takes work to stop that process in my heart!

Letting go of my plans and my perceived control of a situation means I am choosing to believe that God's way is better than my way and that what He wants for me is ultimately better than what I want for me. Choosing to surrender is often a day-by-day or even a second-by-second struggle, as I am so prone to take back the things I give to Jesus and start trying to control them again!

The struggle to enter that place of peace is infinitely worth it though, because living out of that place of rest means I am running on His strength instead of my own, and because finding peace through surrender is key to our calling as women made in His image.

In her book *Thou Givest...They Gather,* Amy Carmichael wrote, "This peace, something we could not possibly have given to ourselves, He gave it to us... Now the enemy has come to cast us out of this that He has given. Can he? If he finds us out of the place of rest and song, he can and he will. But if we are within it, if we want to be within it, then he cannot drive us out of the possession that the Lord of peace did cause us to possess."

The place of rest and song does not just happen. It has to be intentionally entered into. It is holy ground we must fight to maintain. The Enemy cannot steal our peace so long as we remain in that place. Or, to state it another way, our peace can only be stolen if we remove ourselves from that place of rest. We therefore must work to enter into that place of rest, and then choose to remain in the place of rest—the place where I remain ever captivated by my Prince of Peace.

In a world that values accomplishment over communion and productivity over presence, God provided the weapon called *woman* to combat the Enemy's tactics, anchoring us in the present and in His presence, inviting us to live at the pace of abiding rather than the pace of striving, and calling our hearts into peaceful surrender to our King.

> *"She's full of wealth and wisdom."*
> Proverbs 31:10 TPT

Perception

The Spiritual Power of Woman's Intuition

Women are truly so intuitive. I know this "woman's intuition" thing has become a catchphrase, but I was a little late to the full revelation of this because for a long time, I didn't really hang out much with other women—at least not in the sort of trust-filled, honoring, Holy-Spirit focused friendships the Lord meant for us to have with our fellow Proverbs 31 women.

In high school I had one of those best friends where you do everything together and are with each other constantly. I felt inseparable from her (and in all honesty, probably not in the super-healthiest of ways). Long story short, when I stood up against an injustice I saw toward some other girls, my best friend (and all my other friends) ended up turning on me because of it. I still vividly remember reading this "goodbye letter" from my best friend while weeping uncontrollably at the pain of feeling betrayed and rejected for doing what I thought was the right thing. Fast forward to starting college one year later, I was extremely insecure about friendships and effectively held everyone at arm's length so that I couldn't be hurt like that again. Lies from the world weren't helpful either. It didn't take long before I was bombarded with ideas about women being catty and gossipy, and since I was coming out of a place of hurt and insecurity, I eagerly latched onto these lies which gave me something else to blame for why I wasn't able to form close friendships.

> **Through intuition, women can often perceive not only what is right and true, but also what will be the most hurtful.**

Eventually I learned that it isn't true that women are inherently catty and gossipy. That is a lie the Enemy has been whispering with the aim of disrupting healthy relationships among women. (The devil's game is to divide where there should be unity and unite where there should be division). However, any good lie has a little bit of truth sprinkled into it.

I believe women are incredibly intuitive. Through intuition, women can often perceive not only what is right and true, but also what will be the most hurtful. When intuition is used for evil, it can be wielded as an incredibly destructive weapon. Hence there is a sprinkle of truth in the popularized saying: "Hell has no fury like a woman scorned."

On the flip side though, women's intuitive nature can be so powerful in discerning the deep things in our own and others' hearts, allowing us to get to the root of relational issues, systemic problems, and even difficult decisions. I think the reality of how intuitive women are tells us something about the importance of (healthy) vulnerability and honesty in our friendships with godly women, because pretending everything is okay when everything is clearly not okay does not work for more than about two seconds where there's a woman involved! In the context of healthy friendship, this can be so beneficial.

Tension in relationship stems from something being 'off' in my heart, and so if someone who loves me and has my best interests in mind is able to correctly perceive the root of the issue, it gives me an opportunity to take that issue before the Lord and invite Him to do some heart surgery and make me a better person—not just in that relationship or situation but in all my relationships.

Women are perceivers, uniquely equipped to peer into spiritual realities, and our perceiver nature extends far beyond "women's intuition". It is a spiritual reality and another way God uniquely equipped women with a powerful part of His nature. I believe there are several ways that woman's perception is designed to powerfully operate and serve the world for Kingdom purposes, including wisdom, emotional intelligence, and the ability to see potential.

Wisdom

God's wisdom stands in stark contrast to worldly wisdom, which James describes as "earthly, unspiritual, demonic" (James 3:15). Worldly wisdom is rooted in a philosophy of self-sufficiency, causing us to be jealous of others' favor, bitter toward those who have wronged us, and perpetually discontent, living in a state of stressful striving in an attempt to find a satisfaction that forever remains ever so slightly beyond our grasp (James 3:14). Worldly wisdom tells us to put others down to raise ourselves up, not even necessarily in practice but at least in mindset because according to worldly wisdom, thinking of others as insignificant will mask our own feelings of insignificance. It opens the door to a world full of jealousy and selfish ambition which inevitably leads to the degradation of family and community because seeking my own fulfillment at others' expense will eventually present a relationship cost to be paid. Worldly wisdom suffocates relationship because it views every person as either having it better than me (which makes me jealous), having something at my expense (which makes me bitter), or competing with me for the acceptance and validation I think I need in order to form my identity (which makes me selfish).

The problem is that worldly wisdom makes a whole lot of sense in the moment. When someone wrongs me, responding with bitterness seems like an appropriate response. It feels like justice; it feels like I am making the person pay a reasonable price for his or her actions, but the reality is that those reactions are the reactions of worldly wisdom and they only make sense according to worldly culture and not according to Kingdom culture.

By contrast, the wisdom of Kingdom culture is birthed out of eternity (Proverbs 8:22,30), bringing an eternal perspective rather than a temporal one, and it is manifested in meekness.

> *"Who is wise and understanding among you? By his good conduct let him show his works in the meekness of wisdom."*
>
> *James 3:13*

What an amazing picture that is! Meekness is defined as power under control, or power that is properly managed by the person with the power. It is not abdicating authority, but rather knowing how and when it is appropriate (or not appropriate) to exert that authority. It is walking in confidence of one's position, without lording that position over people. It is the quiet confidence of someone who knows who she is and has nothing to prove. Heavenly wisdom's manifestation as meekness (power hidden through restraint) is the exact opposite of worldly wisdom's manifestation, which is strife (weakness attempting to obtain power).

Meekness is the quiet confidence of someone who knows who she is, and has nothing to prove.

Wisdom is manifested from a place of strength. A heart obscured by insecurity will not have the foundation necessary to properly house the spirit of wisdom, because insecurity stemming from self-sufficiency and a mindset of competing with others for one's sense of identity is the soil in which worldly wisdom flourishes, and is diametrically opposed to the atmosphere of purity and peace that heaven's wisdom inhabits.

Women were designed to uniquely manifest God's wisdom. King Solomon, the wisest man (besides Jesus) to have ever lived, personified wisdom as a woman throughout the book of Proverbs. In speaking through the voice of 'Lady Wisdom', who longs to teach people her ways and impart the treasure of wisdom she carries, Solomon seems to indicate that wisdom is an aspect of God that woman reflect in unique ways.

Isn't it interesting that the Enemy has created a sense of competition among women, a tendency to strive against each other for significance and compare ourselves with each other instead of building each other up? These very ingredients are the perfect setup for the manifestation of worldly wisdom; they create an environment that is opposite of that in which heaven's wisdom will thrive. It seems the Enemy knows something he has been trying to keep us unaware of—that women were designed to manifest wisdom.

Satan's strategy is deception. For us as believers, he has no real power over us and so the only card he has to play is the deception card. Unfortunately, he is really good at playing it. He will invest a remarkable amount of time and patience to build a mindset of half-truths that are just believable enough that we easily adopt them into our view of ourselves and the world until we begin incorporating outright lies into our belief systems without realizing we are doing so. According to the rules of the deception game, the best way to trick someone out of their calling is to get them to pursue the counterfeit version of that calling—something that looks and sounds really close to the real deal, something that has just enough truth in it to make us so satisfied with the counterfeit that we give up pursuit of the real thing.

> **The best way to trick someone out of their calling is to get them to pursue a counterfeit version of that calling.**

Hence the Enemy has been presenting women with counterfeit wisdom since the beginning of time. He started with Eve. His message to her was: "You know you were created for X" (the truth) "so therefore you must do Y to make it happen" (the lie). Counterfeit wisdom makes sense to human reason which is why it is so easily accepted. But as the spirit of both wisdom and revelation (Ephesians 1:17), the Holy Spirit gives wisdom through revelation rather than through intellectualism. Counterfeit wisdom tells us to take matters into our own hands, to strive with people and things in the natural to fulfill our destinies and possess our inheritance. By contrast, heavenly wisdom comes out of a place of rest. James says that heaven's wisdom is pure, peaceable, gentle, open to reason, merciful, impartial, and sincere (James 3:17).

I believe the Lord is calling us as women back to the wisdom He created us to carry. If I'm being honest, close relationships with other women have for much of my life felt risky and not worth it. I feared these relationships were only a setup for the inevitable unhealthy competition for validation and acceptance from a perceived limited supply of such resources. But this line of thinking is rooted in counterfeit wisdom, and it is time we called the Enemy on his bluff, exposing counterfeit wisdom for what it is. It is time we cast off strife and competition with each other. It is time we chose to dwell in the place of refuge under the shadow of the Almighty, letting Him alone define us and validate us so we can be free to live in divinely-orchestrated harmony with each other, pooling our wisdom gifts to impart to the world around us the highest form of wisdom we can provide through the collaboration of our shared revelation.

If I'm being honest, close relationships with other women have for much of my life felt risky and not worth it.

This past season for me has been a season of learning to collaborate and develop true friendships with other women. The road hasn't always been easy; we have certainly had our ups and downs, and in many ways the closest friendships I have today were actually born out of the way we walked together through the healing process after having deeply wounded each other. The journey has been infinitely worth it though, as I truly did not know what I was missing before having deep, trusting friendships with other women.

Women are beautiful and powerful, and the more I reap from the wisdom my friends were designed to carry, the more I wish I had not wasted so many years living in fear of doing life with other women. They see things in me (both good and bad) that I can't see in myself and are constantly building me into the best version of me through their wise perceptions. Of the woman connected to her divine purpose and design, Solomon writes:

> *"Her teachings are filled with wisdom and kindness, as loving instruction pours from her lips."*
>
> Proverbs 31:26 TPT

God's ways are so much higher than ours; He has ideas and insights that blow away our wildest imaginations and most creative solutions. Heaven's answers for earthly problems far exceed our grandest expectations, and we as women are uniquely designed to manifest this aspect of His nature to a world in desperate need of solutions and guidance born out of heaven's perspective. We step into it by first casting off worldly wisdom, and then by receiving the free gift of wisdom the Holy Spirit promises to give to those who ask (James 1:5). Next, we can multiply the treasure of wisdom we are privileged to carry by collaborating through the heart of purity, peace, and gentleness in which God's wisdom thrives, in order to build on each other's revelations and pursue the heavenly vision for the problem at hand. Together, we can so powerfully change the world through the spirit of wisdom the Lord imparts to His daughters.

We can powerfully change the world through the spirit of wisdom the Lord imparts to His daughters.

Emotional Intelligence

Emotional intelligence is another manifestation of woman's divinely imparted perceiver-nature. I believe women are innately enabled to identify, understand, cultivate, and mature the emotional makeup of people in a unique way. This isn't to say that women operate out of emotion as a general rule; I think society tends to generalize the underlying truth in a way that can make some of us feel like we must not be the norm. In reality, there are plenty of men who primarily operate intuitively and women who primarily operate analytically. Society's tendency to stereotype doesn't help either, making us believe that perception is the same thing as mode of operation, which is not the case!

Irrespective of our natural processing tendency, I believe that inherent within woman's perceiver nature is an ability to identify emotion, assessing its positive and negative effects and contributions in a given situation. It is a skill set women bring to the table as a part of their perceptive nature and is by no means limited to those who operate intuitively.

More than being a skill set that women offer, emotional intelligence is actually one of the things men *need* from women. Society tells us we have to give other things; society's lie in this area is that when a man does something tangible for us, we have to reciprocate with something tangible—whether it's paying for the next meal or giving a little more of our bodies. But the reality is that men and women are built to give and receive differently. Men don't need to receive back what they give. They need to receive what only a *woman* can give. And what we uniquely give is much less tangible—we give emotional intelligence.

This is something men *need* from us. In the same way we have an innate desire for men to take care of us and serve us tangibly, men need us to take care of them emotionally. It's one of the ways God wired us differently, allowing us to provide for each other's unique needs as men and women.

Emotional intelligence is something that comes easily to us as women, so it can be easy for us to undervalue it. There is a danger in assuming that because something comes easily for us, it must come easily for everyone, but that simply is not true! The things that come easily for you are *most* important for you to share with the world because they are the things God put inside of you that He didn't put inside everyone else the same way.

Emotional intelligence is one of those things that comes easily for women and not necessarily for men, so speaking into emotion is a powerful way we can bless the men in our lives (as well as the women in our lives, because let's face it, even if someone has natural gifting for the task at hand, ministering to oneself is always hard to do!). Putting words to emotion has a powerful way of releasing the hold that negative emotion can generate over someone's life and actions, thereby giving the person back the power to develop and use the emotion for its intended purpose.

Emotions need to not only be identified and given voice to; they also need to be properly developed and matured. God is emotional, but our emotions must line up with His so we respond the way He responds. When our emotion is out of line with His, God certainly challenges us, much as He did in Genesis 4:6 (NLT) when he challenges Cain with the question, "Why are you so angry?" Equally, He will call us out when our emotion is accurate, yet our motivation is wrong. In Luke 10:20 (NLT), for example, Jesus identifies motivation that is out of alignment with heaven when He says, "Don't rejoice because evil spirits obey you, rejoice because your names are registered in heaven."

I long to be intimately acquainted with the heart of God—to rejoice with Him in His joy, to weep with Him in His weeping, to be broken by the things that break His heart, and to respond with anger over the injustice that sparks His anger. I also want to respond out of a place of feeling *His* heart, rather than my own. His emotions are rooted in pure motivations, and it is possible for us to mature our emotion to match the purity of heaven's emotion, transforming human emotion into a powerful accelerator of divine purposes.

In addition to discerning and giving voice to one's emotional state and health, emotional intelligence is also about perceiving and predicting the impact of individual emotional atmospheres coming in contact with each other. This is so important, because life is all about relationships—first with God, and then with the people He gives us to love into the Kingdom or grow alongside in Kingdom living. Every pursuit on earth is accomplished by people and for people. Since God delegated dominion of the earth to humankind and honors the free will He created us with, He seldom steps into our world without the request, prayer, or partnership of a human being. In other words, God chooses to outwork His purposes on earth through humans, and therefore human interaction is vitally important to the accomplishment of His purposes.

It is possible for us to mature our emotion to match the purity of heaven's emotion.

Women have unique perception of the complexities of human interaction, and no organization or endeavor is sustainable without the value for human connectedness that women bring to the table.

Stewarding the Pregnancy: The Ability to see Potential

The ability to see someone's potential is a fundamental aspect of good leadership and an important manifestation of wisdom. Leaders in every area of society ought to be aiming to work themselves out of a job by raising people up to reach their full potential until the only solution is multiplication and expansion. As John Bevere points out in his book, *X: Multiply Your God-Given Potential*, multiplication is the biblical definition of what it means to be faithful. "Whatever He puts in our care, we are to return to Him multiplied," he writes. Jesus emphasized the same principle when he told the parable of the talents (see Matthew 25:14-30).

Multiplication occurs when we intentionally impart an aspect or portion of our gifting to the people we are raising up. When we call out the unique giftings and callings in others, we empower them to take up and expand a move of God in ways that reach beyond our individual calling or ability.

Our ability to recognize and nurture potential is a leadership skill the Lord gave in particular measure to women, and it is one of the things that make women irreplaceable in any leadership team or organization. When we perceive someone's destiny, we see future reality as clearly as if it were present reality and the spiritual realm is shifted through a woman's unshakeable faith in that destiny. I love Dr. Luke's description of the way Jesus' mother Mary was on the lookout for Jesus' calling—she was starting to compile evidence of what exactly it was her son was destined for even while He was still a baby. After the shepherds entered the makeshift delivery room where the newborn King lay in a manger, announcing that angels had suddenly appeared to them to declare Jesus' birth, Luke writes: "Mary treasured up all these things and pondered them in her heart" (Luke 2:19).

> **The spiritual realm is shifted through a woman's unshakeable faith in someone's destiny.**

Similar language is used in Luke 2:51 to describe the way Mary held to the evidence of Jesus' calling after twelve-year-old Jesus was found teaching the teachers in His Father's house during Passover. Spiritual mothering is an aspect of woman's call that encompasses all the ways women were designed to release destiny, but before we can manifest the fullness of spiritual motherhood, we first need that initial perception of untapped potential—a perception I'll call a spiritual "pregnancy".

Mary saw evidence of destiny in the reports of angelic hosts at Jesus' birth, in the prophetic words spoken by a man of God named Simeon and a prophetess named Anna at His circumcision ceremony (see Luke 2:22-38), and in the ways Jesus displayed supernatural wisdom at a young age. Rather than look at these moments with mere curiosity or dismiss them as strange and unexplainable events, Mary perceived the supernatural in these moments and held on to them. In so doing, she carried them with spiritual "pregnancy", waiting for the day when these prophetic moments would fully manifest in future reality.

Mary was chosen to steward the most important pregnancy in all of human history. I believe one of the reasons He chose her was the way He knew she would demonstrate to us as women how to nurture the potential He placed inside the people He brings into our lives. In recent months, the Lord has been teaching me so much about the practicalities of mentoring. I've learned that perceiving the things God has placed inside the individuals He has given me to walk alongside enables me to partner with Him in nurturing the seeds of those giftings and callings so as to instill the courage, strengthen the character, and support the faith of these people until they have the capacity to hold the full measure of what the Lord has in His heart for them.

Women are designed by God to carry physical pregnancies, and this is true also in terms of spiritual realities. God honors the way women carry pieces of His heart for the people He has placed in our lives and when we come into agreement with the beautiful realities He sees, the spiritual realm is stirred. We are designed to carry destinies of people and even of whole nations within our hearts. When we carry them in our hearts, we allow their potential to develop. We prepare them to be birthed into physical reality.

> *"She sets her heart upon a nation and takes it as her own, carrying it within her."*
>
> Proverbs 31:16 TPT

To carry perceived destiny is to believe for it until it manifests. It is a beautiful expression of faith that the Lord honors. Motherhood is not simply a state of being in the natural; it is not contingent upon biological children. Motherhood is an eternal part of the Lord's nature that women reflect to the world and He loves to partner with His daughters through the first phase of spiritual motherhood—the pregnancy. During the pregnancy of incubating destinies, so much is happening behind the scenes. Things are assembled into proper place, life is created out of desolation, and throughout the process, we ourselves are changed more and more into His image.

> **We are designed to carry destinies of people and even of whole nations within our hearts.**

God responds to faith, and when by faith we see God's plans and heart for someone and believe it with the assurance brought by divine perception, heaven responds by invading earth to bring the future into being.

The Power of Perception

The perceptive nature of woman serves as an important bridge between the natural and the supernatural, the physical and the spiritual. Our insight into the spiritual realm gives us access to answers that cannot be found anywhere on earth, and the world is yearning for the realities the spiritual realm reveals.

I have heard many men in healthy relationships with their wives testify to the power of heeding their wife's perceiver-gift. Often the intuitive feeling will be rather vague (as in "I just don't feel right about such-and-such") and so it can take a lot of trust for a husband to yield to his wife's intuition. A wife's intuition may be in regard to timing, other times to do with an unforeseen outcome or unhealthy partnership inherent in the decision at hand, but for as many times as I've heard a man say he felt "saved" by heeding his wife's intuition,

I don't believe I've ever heard a man say he regretted doing so! Just as there are aspects of God's nature inherent in men that require our trust in order for us to allow them to fully manifest, intuition is an aspect of God's nature women were created to carry, and it takes trust in healthy relationship in order for our perceiver-nature to manifest to its fullest.

I love the somewhat surprising story of the woman in 2 Samuel 20 who saved her city from destruction. Joab, the commander of King David's army, was on a mission to capture Sheba, a man who had attempted to start a revolt. When Sheba ran away to Abel Beth Maakah, a "wise woman" from the city perceives that if a battle takes place, her city will be destroyed and many innocent lives will be lost. She therefore goes out to negotiate with Joab and in essence says, "Let's skip the battle; we will kill Sheba and bring his head out to you." Then she goes and does what she said! Acting boldly on her perception and using wisdom to determine a different way of doing things ultimately saved many innocent lives while bringing justice and peace to the kingdom.

Intuition is an aspect of God's nature women were created to carry.

Seeing through God's eyes gives us both a new way of thinking and a new way of life that carries powerful potential to transform the world around us. Peering into situations from heaven's perspective to discern and properly apply eternal truth, access the heart of God for people and situations, and steward revealed future callings and destinies are powerful ways God enabled women to manifest His nature to a world desperately in need of heaven's perspective. Spiritual perception, or "woman's intuition", is therefore one of the most important gifts God gave us to steward for His Kingdom.

"She watches over the ways of her household and meets every need they have." Proverbs 31:27 TPT

Provision

Creating Strong Foundations

In many ways, the role of "provider" has traditionally been attributed to men. I didn't think of myself as having an assignment as a provider or as having anything to contribute in the way of provision. Being on a physician's income, this is maybe a weird misperception to have had! But that's the nature of deception—we modify incongruent things in our life to fit them into the narrative of the deception we are holding to. I think somewhere deep inside of me, I was afraid that my career defied the biblical expectation for women and so I responded by trying to deny my womanhood in order to embrace my career.

The truth is that nothing in the Bible actually goes against my career! The Proverbs 31 woman is quite the entrepreneur, managing the estate while selling her own hand-made clothing line (31:24) and buying land and planting a vineyard to evidently start her own wine-making business (31:16). There is a chance that her entrepreneurial exploits provided the financial stability to free her husband to take on a governmental position and leadership role in the city (Proverbs 31:23).

The gender-based role expectations I incorrectly attributed to the Bible were broken down even further when I discovered, surprisingly, that there are numerous examples in the Bible of men cooking (Genesis 18:7, Genesis 25:29, Judges 6:19, 2 Kings 4:39, Ezekiel 4:12, Matthew 26:19, Luke 22:8-13). Somehow I had this perception that marriage and family would come with the expectation that I should take sole responsibility for cooking, cleaning, and errand running for my household. Given my already busy life, this didn't seem practical. My misperception made me afraid of marriage because of the simple barrier of time management. I figured I didn't have time to be married!

Realizing that God never specified whose paycheck has to be bigger and who does which household chores gave me the freedom to consider that marriage is actually do-able and doesn't need to conflict with the other callings on my life. It also helped me to realize that provision is not gender-specific. One of the names God identifies Himself as is Jehovah-Jireh, the Lord who Provides. I believe from a spiritual standpoint (getting away from finances now), men and women both reflect that aspect of God's nature in equally important ways.

Provision is not gender-specific.

Jehovah-Jireh designed all of us to carry an ever-accessible supply of spiritual resources, and He equally distributes these into the spirit of man and the spirit of woman to aid in the establishment and advancement of His Kingdom. Women in particular were created with an innate propensity to create a sense of belonging, establish a launching place for mission, and tend to the most fundamental needs of those who have been commissioned. All three of these facets are essential to any mission and represent ways that we as women can reflect God's provider nature when we share these Kingdom-building resources with the world around us.

You Belong

Women provide a sense of home. There are so many facets to this reality. First, women create an atmosphere of home by providing a sense of belonging. This, I believe, is one of the important ways women reflect God's provider nature. "Home" is not a destination or a place in the physical, so much as it is a spiritual atmosphere. A woman carries a sense of belonging and acceptance in her heart that enables her to transform the spiritual environment into a place that feels like home.

Hospitality is important in the Kingdom. Firstly, we ourselves can be welcoming homes in which the Holy Spirit can comfortably dwell; and secondly, we can welcome Him to inhabit our houses, workplaces and businesses, and anywhere else we walk into. Hospitality is the invitation to make oneself at home, and the Holy Spirit is forever the number one guest to be invited in. I want my every dwelling place to become His dwelling place. I want myself to be a pure vessel He feels comfortable making Himself at home in, and I also want my place of work to be a place He is welcomed in. God equipped women with the gift of hospitality, first and foremost so that we could be inviters of His presence everywhere we go, and also so that after inviting Him in, we could usher others into the atmosphere of acceptance and belonging that is now inhabited by the Father.

> **God equipped women with the gift of hospitality first and foremost so that we could be inviters of His presence everywhere we go.**

One woman who excelled in creating a sense of belonging was Ruth's mother-in-law, Naomi. Naomi and her husband Elimelech fled to Moab during a time of famine in Israel and their two sons ended up marrying Moabite women. When Naomi's husband and two sons died in Moab, she instructed her daughters-in-law Orpah and Ruth to return to their parents. Neither wanted to return because they felt a stronger sense of belonging with Naomi than they did with their families. I find this incredible! Naomi was from a different culture and religion than what Orpah and Ruth had grown up with. There was also a significant generation gap. Orpah and Ruth were still young and Naomi implied they could both easily remarry and start a new life by returning to their families. From a logical (and financial) perspective, Naomi's advice seems like the obvious choice. Yet something about Naomi makes her feel more like 'home' to these girls than anything they've ever known.

Orpah eventually agreed to return to her people, but Ruth felt such a strong connection to Naomi and Naomi's God that she insisted, "Do not urge me to leave you or to turn back from following you; for where you go, I will go, and where you lodge, I will lodge. Your people will be my people and your God, my God. Where you die, I will die, and there I will be buried. May the Lord do the same to me [as He has done to you], and more also, if anything but death separates me from you" (Ruth 1:16 AMP). It was a hefty vow, and Ruth meant every word.

> "Your people will be my people, and your God, my God." Ruth 1:16

I love that in her vow of devotion to Naomi, Ruth declares she is taking Naomi's God as her own as well. I believe Ruth knew that the sense of love and belonging that Naomi carried originated from God and because of that she was willing to go anywhere and pay any cost to be a part of that divine culture of love she saw in Naomi.

This is what it means to carry the hospitality of the Kingdom. It is a beautiful assignment God uniquely equipped women to carry. In God's Kingdom, everyone who wants to come and be a part is welcome. There are no prerequisites or qualifications other than giving Him our "yes". No one is excluded. God does not see hierarchy or earthly status the way we do (Romans 2:11). His is an upside-down Kingdom in which "the last will be first, and the first last" (Matthew 20:16). The Lord raises up the humble and abases the proud (James 4:6, 10; Proverbs 16:18). He has an entirely different way of evaluating leadership-readiness than our human standards, looking at the hidden places of the heart, the places we can only see by supernatural perception (1 Samuel 16:7). When Jesus walked the earth, the ones who first set foot in His Kingdom were often those who appeared the least likely to do so, but they were willing and ready to say yes and that will forever be the only thing required.

This aspect of Kingdom culture blows the world away, or at least it is supposed to. The watching world is to be able to identify us, not by our fancy programs or even by a specific set of beliefs, but by our love. Jesus said in John 13:35 (NLT), "Your love for one another will prove to the world that you are My disciples." With this idea in mind, Paul urges the Church to "make every effort to keep yourselves united in the Spirit, binding yourselves together with peace" (Ephesians 4:3 NLT). The first-century non-Christian world was amazed by the love the Church had for each other that stretched across human barriers and blew away human prejudices. Jew and Gentile, male and female, slave and free (Galatians 3:28). All were welcome in the Christian community, and the watching world was amazed.

The unity created through the spirit of adoption is another impactful way God equipped women to be creators of Kingdom culture. From the least to the greatest in the world's eyes, ours is to be a community that declares in speech and conveys through the very spirit in the room, "You are wanted and accepted and important to us. You belong here and you are immediately and fully considered one of us. You have nothing to prove and you are just as important to our family as the person who has been here thirty years. We love you for who you are because God loves who you are. We see with His eyes the treasure He put inside of you and we will call out that greatness inside of you until it fully manifests and you are completely aware of the amazing person you are in Him."

> **All were welcome in the Christian community, and the watching world was amazed.**

Such is the empowering message of the spirit of adoption God placed within His daughters for the purpose of expanding Kingdom culture, astounding the watching world, wooing their hearts, and stirring up longing to come and take part in the extravagant, limitless love of God.

It Starts Here

The second provision women give the world is what I like to call "home base". When a man buys a house, it is generally just that—a house. It's a place that provides shelter and serves a purpose, but often there is not much sentimental value in it even if he stays there for an extended time. Bring a woman into the home, however, and a whole new level of identity comes to that place. No longer is it just a place of shelter; no longer is it easily replaced. Women have a way of imparting character and deeply embedding memory into a home in such a way that it becomes inseparable from her touch. Women transform physical buildings into spiritual home bases, and there is something so striking about this phenomenon that it can be easy for us to miss it, or to dismiss it as simply a whimsical aspect of the female nature.

Women transform physical buildings into spiritual home bases.

This natural tendency and ability for woman to create a home base is not an accident. It is a divinely inspired motivation God placed in the heart of woman for Kingdom purposes. All movements need a home base. Even the most widespread companies and the farthest-reaching missionaries need a responsible 'mother business' or church home they can call upon for guidance and support when the need arises. Even in the natural world, we cannot expand our influence and territory without first having a starting place of influence and ownership. Similarly in the spiritual realm, we can't advance the Kingdom without being planted in a place from which our territory can expand. The fullness of Kingdom inheritance is given to those with the capacity to hold it, and women are wired with the capacity to hold the 'more' that God wants to pour out.

One woman who understood the fundamental importance of a home base and who used her womanly gifting in that area in an effective way for the advancement of the Kingdom was a woman named Lydia. Lydia was a businesswoman, a "seller of purple", who lived in the city of Philippi in the first century. When the Apostle Paul and his team traveled to her city in search of those to whom they could share the good news of the gospel, they found that the spiritual heartbeat of the city consisted of a group of women who gathered at the river to fellowship and worship. Among them was Lydia, a woman who worshipped Yahweh (Acts 16:14) but had not yet heard of Jesus. Upon hearing the good news of salvation through Jesus as the promised Messiah who took on Himself the sin penalty of all the world thereby reconciling us to communion with the Lord, Lydia and her household immediately placed their faith in Jesus. Being the businesswoman she was, Lydia understood that a message and movement of this magnitude was going to require a stable launching point from which they could reach her city with the gospel. Her woman's group was a start but it was not enough; Lydia wanted her whole city to be reached with the gospel. So she shared the gospel with her family and then transformed her home into the base from which the Philippian church could advance.

> **Lydia understood that a message and movement of this magnitude was going to require a stable launching point.**

Triumph among the women's group quickly met retaliation from the Enemy who sought to confound Paul's message by associating him with a young girl who used demonic power rather than God's power. When Paul through the anointing of the Holy Spirit finally delivered the girl from the demon, the men who had been exploiting the girl for her demonic divination skills started a riot. This led to Paul and Silas' imprisonment which was then ended abruptly by an angelic jailbreak.

Upon their release, Paul and Silas immediately returned to Lydia's house where the brand-new Philippian church gathered to farewell Paul and his team before they headed out to their next destination (Acts 16:39-40). The text seems to imply that already by this time, the small but growing Philippian church was starting to thrive from the home base Lydia wisely and generously started in her home.

The Philippian church was a church plant that went on to become particularly dear to Paul's heart. These believers were incredibly faithful, supporting Paul through the ups and downs of success and hardship, sticking with him even when he was imprisoned for the sake of the gospel. Lydia's faithfulness to the call to provide a home base therefore not only provided the launching pad for revival in her city, it also provided a source of stability for the Apostle Paul that empowered his mission to a degree that far exceeded the impact of any other supporting church.

Women of the Kingdom, there are many more home bases to start, many more homesteads that are in the heart of the Father and that He wants us as His daughters to catch glimpse of and manifest on the earth—home bases for families, for churches, for ministries, for nonprofits and organizations, for businesses, for conferences, for missions. Every move of God needs a starting place, a launching pad, and He has put it in His daughters to create the multifaceted birthing centers needed for the advancement of His Kingdom in every facet of society. Let's own that assignment, ever expanding our invisible territory and spiritual inheritance until the kingdoms of this world become the Kingdom of our Lord (Revelation 15:11).

Sustenance

Women are wired to fill people up with the energy needed for day-to-day life. In the natural, this often manifests as food provision. In planning for any gathering whether big or small, women are almost always the ones to take responsibility for the menu, and when invited to a woman's home there will almost always be consideration of how food ought to be made available. Men are generally not as quick to volunteer for meal planning, not because they aren't willing to jump in but simply because it is not at the forefront of their minds.

Solomon says of the virtuous woman, "Even in the night season she arises and sets food on the table for hungry ones in her house and for others" (Proverbs 31:15 TPT). There is just something within the heart of woman that can't stand to see people go hungry, no matter how inconvenient it might be to step into the situation as provider. Even physiologically, the Lord created woman's body to provide for her children during pregnancy and after the baby is born, and I believe that those natural tendencies and physical abilities are designed to be reflections of deeper spiritual realities.

Food is used throughout Scripture as a metaphorical representation of spiritual truth. When tempted by Satan in the wilderness to prove Himself by creating physical food, Jesus reminded Himself of truth and reversed the Enemy's lie by declaring that "people do not live by bread alone, but by every word that comes from the mouth of God" (Matthew 4:4 NLT).

Echoing this analogy, Proverbs 31:14 in the Passion translation reads, "She gives out revelation-truth to feed others. She is like a trading ship bringing divine supplies from the merchant." Just as a woman will go to great lengths to ensure food is available to ward off impending hunger in the natural, so will the mighty woman of valor whose heart beats in sync with the Father's go to great lengths to search out the spiritual truth needed to sustain a person's spiritual life. God is the divine supplier; He imparts His sustaining truth in our hearts through His living, active, and powerful word.

> "She gives out revelation-truth to feed others."
> Proverbs 31:14 AMP

> "She watches over the ways of her household and meets every need they have."
>
> Proverbs 31:27 TPT

God has provided everything we need for the life He purposed for us (2 Peter 1:3); we need only to take hold of the spiritual realities He has given and often He will give us more than enough of whatever it is He intends for us to share. Women are adept at recognizing hunger, both in the natural and in the supernatural realms, and the Lord gave us, His daughters, a piece of His provider's heart so we could fill up the hungry places we see in our world. Jesus declared to His disciples, "Blessed are those who hunger and thirst for righteousness, for they shall be satisfied" (Matthew 5:6). It is in His heart to satisfy hunger. Emptiness drives us crazy because it first drives *Him* crazy and because He has given us the means to fill up the empty.

"She stretches out her hand to help the needy", Proverbs 31 proclaims; "...she is known by her extravagant generosity to the poor, for she always reaches out her hands to those in need" (Proverbs 31:19-20 TPT). Filling the empty, satisfying the hungry, providing sustenance for those in need—such is the important call the Lord places within the heart of woman to declare truth in such a way that it speaks new beginnings to barren places, resurrection life to death, hope to hopelessness, mercy to remorse, and redemption to condemnation.

The unique drive the Lord placed within woman's heart to satisfy hunger sets her apart in her specific reflection of His provider-nature, and it is fundamentally important. Physical bodies die without food, and similarly spiritual lives will die without the Word. We need both the written word *(logos)* and the spoken, or now-word *(rhema)*, of the Lord to sustain our spiritual lives and keep us healthy. And so, as daughters of the King and ambassadors in the Kingdom, we have a specific call to receive the life-giving word He brings so we can sustain those He entrusts to us with the spiritual food He gives us to share.

Reflecting the Provider

We have seen that God is Jehovah-Jireh, the Lord God who Provides, and that we reflect His provider nature when we provide as He does. As we provide, we enable others to do the work they are called to do. We don't do the work for people; instead, we equip them with the tools they need to accomplish the work. Just as the Holy Spirit provides the grace-power for us to manifest gifts but will never manifest gifts in an unwilling host, so we must provide the tools needed for the work without forcing work on people. Peter writes, "His divine power has granted to us all things that pertain to life and godliness" (2 Peter 1:3). God has provided all things through the power of His grace, but that doesn't mean we automatically live out abundant life and godliness all the time. We still have to choose to access the things that have been provided. The Holy Spirit provides gifts, but it is up to us to "stir [them] up" (2 Timothy 1:6 NKJV).

In harmony with the Holy Spirit and as women made in the image of the Provider, we offer up the spiritual provisions the Lord deposits into us, and then leave the work itself to be done by those who are called to that work. What people do with our giving out of the abundance of what our Father deposits into us is not up to us. Our responsibility is simply to give out of what has been given to us (Matthew 10:8) and as we do so, we will be given even more to pour out.

> "Give, and you will receive. Your gift will return to you in full—pressed down, shaken together to make room for more, running over, and poured into your lap. The amount you give will determine the amount you get back."
>
> Luke 6:38 NLT

Sister, there are things the Lord has deposited into your spirit that need to be poured out. If we don't give what has been entrusted to us, and instead keep them for ourselves, those things will become stagnant in our hearts and will eventually be no good even for us. It is by giving them away that we unleash rivers of provision in the spirit and access an unending supply of spiritual resources. The more we release joy into others, the more the joy of the Lord is deposited into us; the more peace we impart, the more peace is imparted to us; and the more unconditional love we pour out to those around us, the more the Father establishes us on the firm foundation of His love for us.

The release of spiritual floodgates made possible through giving of our spiritual inheritance is made possible only by His Spirit. "Not by might, nor by power, but by My Spirit," the Lord says to Zerubbabel (Zechariah 4:6), and His message for us is the same. We give out of what He provides. And as we do, He provides even more for us to steward and distribute for His glory.

"She has no fear of winter for her household, for everyone has warm clothes." Proverbs 31:21 NLT

Protection

Guarding Spiritual Families

Family is so important to the Father's heart. As Christians, our primary identity is as sons and daughters of God. We are not primarily wives, mothers, doctors, teachers, assistants, or ministers; all of these things describe calling, but calling is not identity and there is no way to thrive in a calling without first thriving in identity.

Romans 8:14-16 says, "For all who are led by the Spirit of God are sons of God. For you did not receive the spirit of slavery to fall back into fear, but you have received the Spirit of adoption as sons, by whom we cry, Abba! Father!" I think this verse correlates well with John 15:15 where Jesus tells His disciples: "No longer do I call you servants, for the servant does not know what his master is doing; but I have called you friends, for all that I have heard from my Father I have made known to you." In our spiritual walk, we often progress from a servant-mindset to an understanding of our relationship as sons or daughters and friends.

In my own life, one of the barriers that kept me from embracing my place in His family was perfectionism. My perfectionism kept me bound in a slave-master relationship with God when He was trying to call me out into deeper relationship as His daughter and friend. Servanthood requires only my obedience, not the responsibility to employ the wisdom and gifts He has given to effectively partner with Him in making decisions and taking action. The reality is, it takes more faith to be a daughter and a friend than it does to be a servant, and for so long I was afraid of the freedom that comes with being daughter and friend because I didn't trust myself with the responsibility that comes with freedom.

> **It takes more faith to be a daughter and a friend than it does to be a servant.**

How thankful I am to Jesus for taking me through a long process to kill my attachment to the various things I was placing my identity in by trying to be "perfect" at them (school, work, friendship, romance, etc.). It was only after He stripped those things away and all that was left was Him and me, that He could show me that my true identity is my multifaceted relationship with Him, not just as servant but also as daughter, friend, ambassador, priest, and king.

Knowing and embracing my identity as a daughter of the King in God's family is foundational to my call as a woman because I cannot give of what I do not have. If I don't first embrace my own identity as God's daughter, I won't be able to help others embrace that identity. Our relationship to God and especially with regard to our position in God's family is our only true source of identity. Placing identity in anything else creates a shaky foundation for life and day-to-day ministry and leads us to attempt to advance His Kingdom from a place of trying to prove ourselves rather than from a place of having already received irrevocable approval.

Guarding the family is therefore an incredibly important assignment, and it is one the Lord especially equipped women to carry out. It is an assignment we are not to take lightly because heavenly family is both foundational to human identity and something our Father-King holds so very close to His heart.

Defending Self

The Lord equipped women with the instinct and ability to defend communities. But before we can protect others, we must first ensure we ourselves are on stable ground, that we operate from a place to which we can bring others for safety and support.

Self-protection is a difficult topic to tackle. It is easy to reduce the concept to hiding ourselves behind insurmountable invisible walls built by offense having given way to bitterness. From personal experience, this is one I have definitely learned the hard way! While one of the barriers that kept me from embracing my identity as God's daughter was perfectionism, the other was my unhealthy interpretation of self-protection. Relationships with people who didn't understand either their own identity as God's child or God's definition of me as a woman led to hurts that I allowed to fester into bitterness. The Bible warns about the way unforgiveness can turn into a "root of bitterness" (Hebrews 12:15 NKJV) and the danger of allowing it to take root in our hearts is that it can become so prevalent that we actually believe it is meant to be there. "I just don't trust people easily," I would tell myself. "That's just who I am." *False!* It is not who I am. At one time I did have an ability to trust, but I had become defensive and walled-off, not out of wisdom, but rather out of bitterness and unforgiveness.

> **Before we can protect others, we must first ensure we ourselves are on stable ground.**

Such self-protection is not the same as healthy self-care. It can take a lot of diving deep with the Holy Spirit to distinguish the difference in our hearts and allow Him to heal the unhealed hurts that the bitter roots are growing out of. When we build insurmountable walls, we hide our true identities and rob the world of the joy of knowing us and benefiting from the world-changing things we can offer.

This is why we need to be on stable ground in order to bring stability. The wondrous thing about our faith is that we fight from a place of victory. Similarly, we empower from a place of being empowered, we love from a place of having received love, and we provide safety and stability from a place of being covered ourselves.

The Proverbs 31 woman is said to ensure her household is properly clothed: "She has no fear of winter for her household, for everyone has warm clothes" (Proverbs 31:21 NLT), but she is also noted to herself have clothing that is beautifully fashioned together (Proverbs 31:22). She herself is covered, and this is what enables her to provide covering for her family.

I love this idea of covering. It reminds me of Psalm 91:1: "He who dwells in the shelter of the Most High will abide under the shadow of the Almighty." When we give ourselves to the Lord, we receive His covering. He shelters, protects, and defends us. When slander, jealousy, manipulation, and outright evil come against us or the plans the Lord has for our lives, He is the covering under which we are safe. I believe this is the important difference between unhealthy and healthy covering. Self-covering that is created by me is unhealthy, whereas covering created by allowing God to be my defense is healthy. I can't foresee every possible situation, and therefore if I'm going to effectively protect myself by my own efforts, it usually will result in closing myself off and guarding myself so excessively that I can't have real friendships and relationships. If on the other hand I let God, who is able to see the future and "search the hearts" (Romans 8:27, Jeremiah 17:10) of people, guide me and give me wisdom as to who to let into my heart and who to avoid connection with, I won't have to live in fear. Instead, I can live in sweet intimacy with the people He has brought into my life while

> **When we give ourselves to the Lord, we receive His covering.**

avoiding connection with those He wants to protect me from.

Covering for Self

Ensuring we have covering for ourselves is twofold. First and foremost, our covering is directly from the Lord, and therefore He is the one we ultimately go to for that covering. Being covered by Him requires letting Him into the deep places of our hearts so that He can examine, expose, and purify impure motives and false sources of security that make us vulnerable to the onslaught of deception, accusation, temptation, and despair.

The second aspect of having covering for ourselves involves allowing the Lord to provide and minister to us through those He places in a position to speak into our lives. To remain spiritually healthy, we need to have people in our lives that we minister to, as well as people who minister to us. We all—even those of us who are pastors or teachers or ministers—need to have pastors or mentors who are pouring into us.

> **To remain spiritually healthy, we need to have people in our lives that we minister to, as well as people who minister to us.**

I believe every relationship should have elements of both ministering and being ministered to. No matter how great a spiritual leader is, that person is still human and there is something God can use you to speak to them about. On the flip side, no matter how much you think your mentee needs you, there will be times when that person blows you away by ministering to you with just the right word in just the right season. This give and take keeps us in a place of humility when it comes to those we pour into, and a place of exalting Jesus rather than humans when others pour into us.

Proverbs tells us that an abundance of wise counselors provides success (Proverbs 15:22), safety (11:14), and victory (24:6). We were not meant to be independent. We were meant to live life from a place of dependence—first and foremost on Him, and secondly on His body because as members of His body, we cannot survive without the other members.

In pursuit of our secondary covering through other members of the body, it is important to ask ourselves: Do we have friends who ask us the hard questions and aren't afraid to challenge us? Do we allow their challenging questions to examine our own hearts rather than becoming defensive? If you do not currently have friends like that, I encourage you to ask the Lord to provide you with some tough-love friends! We all need people in our lives who love us enough to fiercely protect the purity of our relationship with the Lord, even if doing so means asking us the tough questions—like whether we are allowing situations that have even the slightest chance of leading us to compromise by offering us unhealthy validation from a human or by enabling someone else to gain unhealthy validation from us.

Another of those tough questions may be asking us to examine if there is anything in our lives we are in bondage to. Bondage is a hard thing to detect; it is found in the subtle unrest that comes from adopting someone else's calling or taking a responsibility that isn't mine to carry. For those of us who easily take on responsibility whenever we see a need, it can be hard to let something die because of someone else's neglect. But this is exactly what we need to do if it is outside our calling, because the more we devote ourselves to keeping someone else's vision alive for them, the more tendency we allow for our own dreams and visions to die without even realizing it. In the end, trying to live out someone else's call because of that person's failure to carry it out results in two dead destinies, and zero fulfilled callings. But these things are often hard to detect when we are smack dab in the middle of it! That is why we need other members of the body to provide the protective covering that keeps us healthy.

I have not always had these kinds of friendships, but am so grateful for the ways the Lord has brought these iron-sharpening-iron (Proverbs

27:17) relationships in this past season. There have even been several times when the Lord has tried to convict me of something and I've been stubborn about it, and I've found that His next approach has been to tell me to talk to those friends! I know when He says it, what He means is "I trust them to tell you the same thing I'm telling you without softening anything because they love you enough to tell you the truth. So ask them and see what they have to say about it." I then go talk to them and sure enough, they tell me the exact thing the Holy Spirit was trying to tell me—the same word that I was trying to ignore. These are my people, not because I always feel "good" around them (being rebuked by the Holy Spirit through someone else doesn't necessarily feel good!) but because I am always loved by them even when loving me means the "tough love" of bringing me into alignment with what is true and right and good for my heart.

Defending the Family

Women are defenders of families. While men often detect outside dangers long before we as women are aware of them, women are uniquely attuned to detect the inside threats against the family unit. In the broken world we live in, there may be many of us who truly do not have the possibility of communing with biological family and to those for whom this is the case, I first want to assure you that there is a greater, spiritual family that we are adopted into through Christ and that you as a woman are still uniquely qualified to defend. But let's dive in for a minute to talk about physical families.

Women are uniquely attuned to detect threats against the family unit.

So many of us have unfortunately been hit by the devastating effects of brokenness within our physical families. Whether it is divorce or unfaithfulness or betrayal or neglect or abuse or death, I would venture to say it is an extremely rare person who has not been affected in some way by the devastating impact of a broken family.

Families have been on the Enemy's radar ever since the creation of the very first family unit. Right at the beginning of Genesis we see the devil capitalizing on Cain's jealousy and encouraging him in his anger and hatred until Cain rose up to commit murder—the murder of his brother, Abel. When God brought Adam and Eve together, a mighty union took place: two people were united into one (see Genesis 2:24).

This uniting of two people through marriage is not to be taken lightly. It creates a powerful force that deserves protection, and in honor of the supernatural transaction that marriage is, the mighty woman of valor and destiny Solomon describes in Proverbs 31 prioritizes her relationship with her husband.

> "Her husband can trust her, and she will greatly enrich his life. She brings him good, not harm, all the days of her life."
>
> Proverbs 31:11-12 (NLT)

Later on, verse 23 seems to imply that she is behind her husband's promotion and respected reputation as a leader in their city as well. In other words, this woman is for her husband and for their marriage. She works hard to build him up and strengthen him, understanding that becoming passive will inevitably lead to the demise of the relationship. Like our relationship with the Lord, the oneness of two people bonded through marriage takes work to maintain. But when the oneness of marriage is maintained through the additional oneness with the Lord as individuals separately and as a couple together, an undefeatable force is created.

> "And though a man might prevail against one who is alone, two will withstand him – a threefold cord is not quickly broken."
>
> Ecclesiastes 4:12

PROTECTION

Marriage has been the unfortunate source of deep heartache for so many, but it also has the potential to be an incredibly effective union with multiplied Kingdom authority, enabling us to overcome and accomplish much more than we could on our own. Those of us who are a part of an earthly marriage have the opportunity and special assignment from the Lord to protect and defend this unique oneness so it can be released as the spiritual weapon it is.

The woman after God's heart pours into her husband and also protects her children, ensuring "everyone has warm clothes" (Proverbs 31:22 NLT) for the winter ahead. She "smiles at the future [knowing that she and her family are prepared]" (Proverbs 31:25 AMP) and in response, "her children stand and bless her [and] her husband praises her" (Proverbs 31:28 NLT). A solid family unit is an empowering, unstoppable force. Like marriage, family in general has been the brunt of so much Enemy onslaught throughout history and in our world today, but God is the God of redemption and no person or situation is beyond His power to redeem and restore. He is the God of prodigal sons returning, the God of families restored.

> **A solid family unit is an empowering, unstoppable force.**

For those of us blessed with family, we have a responsibility to see our families as good things from the Lord, to defend against the little everyday threats that have potential to escalate and sever the unity (Song of Solomon 2:15), and to partner with Him in making family a launching pad for the move of God He wants to happen in our midst. And for all of us, regardless of earthly marital status or family situation, our oneness with Jesus through the Holy Spirit and unity with the Father as daughters of God are even more weighty transactions that deserve our utmost attention to maintain and fiercely protect.

Defending Spiritual Families

Community is powerful. God Himself is a community, comprised of Father, Son, and Holy Spirit, and He designed us to need and thrive in community as well. The Lord promises to show up in the midst of two or more people who gather in His name (Matthew 18:20), and He warns us to not neglect our need to come together for spiritual edification and exhortation (Hebrews 10:25).

Many of us have perhaps been hurt by the devastating wounds of broken family. I want to encourage our hearts that whatever wounds our biological families may have passed down, when we place our faith in Jesus our heavenly Father adopts us into a greater family.

> *"You received God's Spirit when he adopted you as his own children."*
>
> Romans 8:15 NLT

Where earthly parents fail, the Lord steps in as Father to the fatherless. Where marriages are broken, He steps in to personally defend those hurt by the wreckage (Psalm 68:5). The heart of our Father is to bind up the brokenhearted and create the safe refuge of family for those who are alone. Psalm 68:6 (NLT) says that "God places the lonely in families." Our earthly families may have failed to reflect our heavenly family the way they were meant to, but those earthly families were never meant to replace the spiritual family we were designed for. No brokenness on earth can ever negate the heavenly family His grace empowers us to become a part of.

As believers, we are invited into the community of the Trinity that has existed since eternity past.

In our heavenly family, God is our Father, and as His children, we are heirs of God and co-heirs with Christ (Romans 8:17). How amazing is that?! We inherit the same inheritance that belongs to Jesus. John 17:23 is even more mind-blowing, stating that God the Father loves us, His children, in the same way, and with as much love as He loves Jesus. God is love (1 John 4:8), and as believers, we are invited into the community of the Trinity that has existed since eternity past and are privileged to experience the same love that characterizes the very essence of God.

Our unity with the Father, friendship with the Son, and communion with the Spirit (John 15:15; 2 Corinthians 13:14) deserve to be protected, as do our relationships with our fellow co-heirs. God has placed us in His family, and He so deeply wants each of us to experience the empowering and uplifting covering of a healthy spiritual family.

Family is so important to our Father's heart, and women are tasked with the important assignment of defending God's family. Like any earthly family, God's family is comprised of people with all sorts of backgrounds, experiences, and personalities, and maintaining the types of relationships that enable us to empower one another is not a task to be taken lightly!

The woman of Proverbs 31 is introduced at the beginning of the passage as a "virtuous" woman (Proverbs 31:10, KJV). The Passion translation of this verse says she is "a woman of strength and mighty valor." What an amazing description! Women of destiny are mighty warriors, and they protect, as the word implies, through strength, wealth, and wisdom. As defenders of spiritual families, we are on the lookout for division within the body. The greatest threats against the family unit are not external threats; in fact, external threats often bring family together. Instead, the internal threats are most dangerous and are exactly what women are most adept to discern and address. Women have inherent, God-given intuition, and the atmosphere shift associated with the beginning stages of a breech in relationship can often be detected by a woman before outward signs of discord appear.

Maintaining healthy relationships with other members of our spiritual family requires the hard work of vulnerability, confession, and accountability. Confessing our sins to each other (James 5:16) deflates the power of that sin over our lives and sets us free. Similarly, vulnerability through trust, accountability, and an honest assessment of both our victories and our shortcomings, helps us remember who we truly are as children of our heavenly Father.

Women naturally detect when there is an offense to be confessed, a debt to be forgiven, or a breech in relationship to be repaired. Going after these tough issues is often uncomfortable and may not be our favorite assignment, but it is so important! So many aspects of God's character can only be learned through relationships with other people, and that often means going through the tough work of reconciliation. I have never regretted a nudge from a trusted friend to address a breech in relationship with another person, and I have never regretted being the pusher either! Good friends will pick up on relational tension and say something along the lines of, "Hey, I feel like something is going on with you and so-and-so? I don't need to know the details but whatever it is, go fix it!"

These nudges certainly need to be done in love with the right heart, yet it is important to remember that staying silent can be so much more harmful than speaking up because unspoken offense enables a root of bitterness to take hold. Left unchecked, it will ultimately destroy a person's friendships, ministry, and fellowship with the Lord. As root-of-bitterness weeders, we must remember that we ourselves are just as capable of being trapped in bitterness as those we detect bitterness in. Bitterness always feels like a just response, but human justice is not to be compared to the justice system of the Righteous Judge and is never worth the cost of usurping the work of justice He can do on our behalf.

Repairing the breeches is how we guard against the deadly internal threats of unforgiveness, bitterness, offense, and resentment in a family. The Scripture points out that disrupted relationship with other people is one of the specific reasons our prayers may not be answered

(Matthew 5:24; 11:25). We cannot overestimate how important family is to Him! We also cannot overestimate how important our assignment is to guard God's family against the internal disruptors of the love that is inherent in the Trinity and graciously lavished on us as His children. Women of destiny, we must own well our assignment to protect the precious relationships of spiritual family.

Covering in Family

I love the idea of covering. Being covered conveys a sense of safety and protection. It gives the message, "I've got your back!" As our heavenly Father covers us (see Psalm 91:1), we are instructed to likewise cover each other. 1 Peter 4:8 tells us, "Above all, keep loving one another earnestly, for love covers a multitude of sins." When you are covered by love, you don't have to worry about making mistakes. You don't have to worry about doing everything perfectly. When you are covered, you can advance the Kingdom and push back the darkness with confidence, knowing someone has your back and is ready to take out the Enemy forces you don't see. Covering gives us freedom to embrace life with arms wide open, fearlessly pursuing our gifts and callings.

> **"Above all, keep loving one another earnestly, for love covers a multitude of sins." 1 Peter 4:8**

Covering is what family does. It enables us to sidestep the landmines and reach our destinies. 1 Corinthians 13:7 (TPT) reads, "Love is a safe place of shelter, for it never stops believing the best for others. Love never takes failure as defeat, for it never gives up." We need family ties with fellow sons and daughters of God that provide a "safe place of shelter" through a love from the Lord that always wants more for us, and never gives up on us. That kind of covering is the culture of God's family, and it provides the mighty protection needed for us to thrive in all our Father has for us.

One of the devil's most pervasive tactics is to isolate; he knows that we are stronger together and weaker on our own. He also knows that disrupting our family identity threatens the very essence of our sense of self and purpose, because our primary identity is as sons and daughters of God. Jesus made it a point to reveal God as Father, understanding that the revelation of the Father is the basis for our identity as children. If we don't know God as Father then we can't possibly know ourselves, and if we don't know ourselves, we will never experience the fullness of the abundant life God has for us.

Being invited into God's family is the heart of the gospel. Our position in God's family defines, protects, and empowers us. Ensuring each family member is experiencing the fullness of his or her covering is therefore so important. The woman of destiny in Proverbs 31 is said to provide clothing or covering for herself (31:22), but also for her family (31:21). The Passion Translation dives into the spiritual aspect of what covering entails. It reads: "She is not afraid of tribulation, for all her household is covered in the dual garments of righteousness and grace" (Proverbs 31:21).

Righteousness and grace are protective spiritual coverings. The righteousness of Jesus protects us from judgment, and as Peter reminds us, our love for each other can provide protection against the negative effects of sin (1 Peter 4:8). Righteousness is our defensive protection; grace is our offensive protection. Grace enables us to do what we could not do on our own, starting with salvation and then continuing on in every aspect of our walk with God. Grace empowers us to love with His love, preach with His truth, and manifest gifts by His Spirit. And it is by grace that we are enabled to avoid sin, deny the flesh, and conquer the devil. When I truly understand and live out of a place of grace, I am prepared for anything—I am protected from the Enemy and from sin by His impenetrable covering of grace.

Righteousness is our defensive protection; grace is our offensive protection.

PROTECTION

Family provides the priceless gift of covering. As women, we are uniquely designed to cultivate the family of God's Kingdom, ensuring no one is left alone, vulnerable to the schemes of the devil through isolation. We are stronger together, as a people on mission together, holding fast to our King's vision and remaining close to our Father's heart. As women, it is as we cultivate and protect family that God's children can fearlessly pursue their God-given dreams by the power of His grace.

"She considers a field before she buys or accepts it [expanding her business prudently]; With her profits she plants fruitful vines in her vineyard." Proverbs 31:16 AMP

Prophetic Processing

The Destiny-Releasing Power of Woman

The invitation God extends to partner with Him in bringing His Kingdom to earth is something I have only recently started to understand, and I am amazed by the privilege and authority He gives us as humans to "take dominion" (Genesis 1:26,28) and rule over the earth. As we come alongside Him through prayer and declarations as well as through walking out our gifts and callings, we partner with Him for His will to be done on earth just as it is done in heaven (Matthew 6:10). To do this, we need discernment to process revelation and instruction from the Lord. This requires us to distinguish between human responsibility and the responsibility that inherently belongs to the Lord.

God is sovereign, but He also tells us plainly that His will is often not done on the earth (if it were, we would not see so much brokenness in the world!). There are countless actions on earth that God will not do Himself because He has given them to us to do. We sadly relinquished our authority for several thousand years after Eden, but thanks be to Jesus who as the second Adam, both fully God—and importantly, fully human—broke the curse, and as the Son of Man won back for us the authority that the first man Adam had relinquished.

Because of the authority Jesus won back for us on earth, we have a responsibility to give God our surrender and obedience in order to facilitate the manifestation of something He has declared over us or our circumstances. In his book, *Prophetic Company: The joyful journey toward building prophetic community*, Dan McCollam writes, "Wise spiritual mothers and fathers help us not only rightly interpret prophetic words, but also come alongside in walking out the often challenging distance between process and promise".

Both spiritual mothers and fathers have an assignment to come alongside spiritual sons and daughters and help them process the things God has spoken over their lives. But there are aspects of this assignment that pertain specifically to us as spiritual mothers. Back in Eden after the first man received the breath of life and before the woman was fashioned into existence, God pointed out the void He perceived in a world without women and gave brief commentary revealing that He created woman with the specific intention of filling that void: "Then the LORD God said, 'It is not good for the man to be alone. I will make a helper who is just right for him'" (Genesis 2:18 NLT).

> "Wise spiritual mothers and fathers . . . come alongside in walking out the often challenging distance between process and promise."
> – Dan McCollam

The choice of the word "helper" is so interesting because throughout Scripture it is used to describe God. It also carries the idea of protection. "All you who fear the LORD, trust the LORD! He is your helper and your shield" (Psalm 115:11 NLT), the psalmist writes, and numerous other passages use the word to describe God helping His people defeat their enemies and remain in safety (see Deuteronomy 33:7, Psalm 33:20, Exodus 18:4). On the flip side, warning is given to God's people when they refuse to receive protective help from God: "He destroys you, O Israel, for you are against me, against your helper" (Hosea 13:9).

This defending and preserving help of God is so important! When God declares a thing, our Enemy immediately starts planning the interruption of that thing and we need God's defending, warfare-ready help to protect that declaration through to its manifestation. God gave woman a specific capacity and assignment to carry His helper-nature, preserve and protect His declarations against Enemy onslaught, and release the destiny God has spoken.

The word 'help' can also refer to giving assistance or support, to furthering the advancement of a task or project. Help enables us to complete a task at hand more efficiently than we would have without assistance. God gave Adam and Eve a mandate to take dominion over the earth (Genesis 1:28) and as *helper*, the woman was to bring an added efficiency and effectiveness in carrying out this mandate. Put together, the call

The call to be a helper is a call to facilitate, enhance, and propel the purposes of God.

to be a helper is therefore a call to facilitate, enhance, and propel the purposes of God, as well as to do battle with the Enemy when he comes against the things God has spoken. As divinely-appointed helpers, women are uniquely equipped to bring forth God's rule on the earth.

As women, our perceptive nature allows us to carry the "pregnancy" of destinies for people, businesses and even whole nations, shifting the spiritual atmosphere by faith, because faith stirs heaven to action. But our influence doesn't end there—women are also equipped to birth those perceived spiritual realities into the physical, to call the unseen into the seen, the future into the now. Proverbs 31:16 (AMP) says the woman of valor "considers a field before she buys it or accepts it [expanding her business prudently]; With her profits she plants fruitful vines in her vineyard." As women of wisdom, we evaluate potential new territory to step into, and then when we discern the promise is from God, we not only buy or own the promise, we also develop it.

Women tend to take what they have and multiply it into something more, making a fertilized egg into a baby, a house into a home, a field into a garden. The same phenomenon occurs when we "incubate" our prophetic perceptions, developing them until they are ready to be "birthed" into reality. When we prophesy our divinely-inspired perceptions and rise to action through the unique influence of a woman, new realities come into being.

There are destinies that cannot be realized without a woman's touch, spiritual realities that won't come to be unless a woman releases them.

There are destinies that cannot be realized without a woman's touch, spiritual realities that won't come to be unless a woman releases them.

The Lord gives vision to both His sons and daughters, but along the path toward realizing the vision, there are pieces of the process He gives to His daughters to unlock. This is why the first word God used to describe woman is "protective helper". Women protect vision, defend promise, and facilitate destiny. God paused the creation of the universe in Genesis 2 to declare the world's need for women because women facilitate the process to fulfill God-given purpose.

Women are destiny catalysts!

The Power of Trust

As women we have a powerful destiny-releasing weapon at our disposal, and because it is so effective, it often comes under attack. This important weapon in our arsenal is our *trust*.

There is something wonderfully inspiring about having earned the trust of a strong, confident woman. A woman assured of her unique calling and influence as a woman, at rest in her God-ordained femininity, comfortable in her own skin; a woman who doesn't *need* you to take notice, but receives the noticing with grace and poise when it comes. Woman's trust is an effective enabler for both men and women, but men, in particular, were designed by God to be propelled by woman's trust. Of the woman of Proverbs 31 it is said that "her husband can trust her, and she will greatly enrich his life" (Proverbs 31:11 NLT). I believe the commentary about her husband's position toward the end of the chapter is also a tribute to her, demonstrating that her trustworthiness and faithfulness to her husband empowered him with the confidence and courage he needed to become a leader in their city: "Her husband is well known at the city gates, where he sits with the other civic leaders" (Proverbs 3:23 NLT). When a man receives genuine and uninhibited trust from a woman like that, there is nothing he can't do. He is suddenly empowered to fight for justice, to protect the vulnerable, and to live out his destiny.

> "Her husband can trust her, and she will greatly enrich his life." Proverbs 31:11 NLT

For this reason, we ought to value our trust as the precious gem it is, respect the force it is, and ensure it is not harmed. Our trust is not meant for just anyone—it must be earned; no question about it. Trust is never a free gift. It is a weapon that must be wielded carefully. This is why we must be careful to guard our trust because when trust is abused by someone who is not worthy to carry it, it can compromise the impact of that trust, limiting the ways we can empower those who are actually worthy of it—at least until the trust is healed, which takes time.

However, while overusing our trust weapon can be detrimental, underutilizing it can be equally devastating. While trust has to be earned and should not be given away freely, the flip side is this: refusing to give trust to someone who *has* earned it has consequences that are just as serious, because woman's trust has a way of releasing destiny, and I believe the world is full of unrealized destinies still waiting to be released or accelerated by woman's trust.

The sad reality is that trust is so easily compromised, and when trust is compromised (particularly by someone with early or positional prominence in our lives such as a father or father-figure, first boyfriend, or husband) it can take years of God's gentle pursuit for us to allow Him in to heal those parts of us and reinstate our ability to trust. Broken trust has consequences far beyond us, most importantly and immediately for the men in our lives. A man who knows his woman doesn't trust him cannot fulfill his destiny. Woman's trust is one of the things God created man to *need* from woman, because woman's trust, given from a place of purity, allows him to participate in divine purposes—protecting the vulnerable, defending justice, and standing for righteousness. When God places someone in my life who genuinely earns my trust, it is my responsibility to give it, and thereby propel His purposes.

I believe that in so many ways, the world is waiting for woman's trust to be healed. The Enemy has created a culture that quickly steals woman's trust. The Enemy knows the impact of woman's trust, and he will go to great lengths to bring into our lives all kinds of people who are not worthy of our trust, so that by the time we meet someone who is worthy, we are too afraid to give it, and therefore hold back the destiny-releasing, justice-propelling, protection-inspiring effect of woman's trust.

Your trust is one of the most powerful things you carry. It is one of the most potent ways you can empower a man to take his place in his family, his community, and the world; it is the most effective way woman can propel man into his destiny.

Mothering the Destiny

I believe there are two primary modes of operation by which our trust or faith in someone's future can release destiny. First, women 'mother' and nurture destinies into being. Nurturing is an inherent aspect of God's nature that He equipped women to reflect to the world, and the Father's nurturing heart reflected through our assignment of spiritual motherhood is meant to provide the security and consistency foundational to the confident release of destiny.

In her book, *Own Your Assignment: Every Woman's Call to Raise Up World Changers*, Bethany Hicks discusses the importance of understanding spiritual motherhood as an *assignment* to women, taking unique expressions in accordance with our unique personalities and relationships. She writes, "we are no longer *only* daughters and sisters but are *also* called to be mothers. Every woman has the opportunity to step into this assignment because it is the natural trajectory of family maturity and blessing".

> "We are no longer only daughters and sisters; we are also called to be mothers." - Bethany Hicks

Biological children are not a prerequisite for spiritual mothering, neither does marital status in any way affect the assignment every woman has to be a spiritual mother. If there are people in your sphere of influence whose destinies need to be released by a mother's touch, then you might just be the person to mother them into their calling.

The call to motherhood is a call to convert spiritual potential to physical reality at the opportune season. It is an important assignment and carries with it the potential to empower the destinies of people, organizations, and nations.

The Prophetess Deborah was this kind of empowering mother to Israel and Israel's leaders. She owned her assignment well, understanding the impact she had on her nation through her spiritual motherhood. "The villagers ceased in Israel; they ceased to be until I arose; I, Deborah, arose as a mother in Israel" (Judges 5:7).

Deborah explains how she carried Israel's leaders in her heart, reflecting the perceptive nature of woman: "My heart goes out to the commanders of Israel who offered themselves willingly among the people" (Judges 5:9). From that posture of faithfully and lovingly carrying these leaders in her heart, Deborah wins the right to speak into them and release their destinies. "Up! For this is the day in which the Lord has given Sisera into your hand," she declares to Barak (Judges 4:14). Barak asks her to go with him, and she agrees. She doesn't criticize him for it. Barak needs a spiritual mother and Deborah gracefully steps up to mother him into his destiny.

> **From the posture of faithfully and lovingly carrying these leaders in her heart, Deborah wins the right to release their destinies.**

For a long time I undervalued the nurturing and mothering aspects of womanhood; 'mothering' didn't sound like a positive in my mind. I think sometimes the influence of society and even our own experiences can affect the way we view the various aspects of our unique calling as spiritual mothers. I'm sure my perfectionism played quite a role in my misperception because as a young perfectionist, following the rules was what my entire identity was based on! So for the longest time, I didn't understand what mothers are meant to do. I had this perception that mothering involves enforcing rules and in essence holding people back and holding myself back when in reality, mothers do the opposite—they are designed to propel and release destiny.

Jesus didn't need a cautious rule-enforcer; He was born with perfect motives and actions. But Jesus still needed a mother. He needed someone who would carry in her heart the prophetic words spoken over Him (Luke 2:19), and then perceive and call out the time for their fulfillment in order to propel Him into those promises (John 2:3-11). For thirty years, Mary patiently and faithfully carried the words spoken by angels and shepherds, by a man of God named Simeon and a prophetess named Anna (Luke 2:15-38), waiting expectantly for the proper time for her son's destiny to be revealed. She stewarded revelation well and as a good mother, she was ready to release those prophetic words when the time was right.

As the time seemed to draw closer, Mary's spiritual senses were heightened to the approaching season, and she began watching continually for the God-ordained opportunity in which Jesus' calling could start to manifest. She was watching expectantly—even at social gatherings with friends, even at a wedding in Cana. And it was there, at a wedding party surrounded by friends that Mary saw opportunity align with the spiritual season, and she stepped up to call it out.

Mary presents the opportunity-lending problem: "They have no wine" (John 2:3). Jesus knows what she is asking. I imagine them exchanging knowing glances in that moment, Mary silently telling Him that as His mother she has stewarded each prophetic word about her son and carried them to full maturity, and she knows the time has come. Maybe she spoke more out loud than is recorded, or maybe Jesus saw all this in her eyes. Either way, Jesus looks at her and agrees with her spiritual perception as she calls it out: The time is *now*. It is time for His ministry to go public, time for Him to step fully into the calling on His life, time for Mary to fulfill her call as His mother through releasing the prophecies spoken over Him.

Mary sees that Jesus agrees, and with the confidence of a woman who knows her long-awaited destiny-propelling call of motherhood is about to be fulfilled, she declares to the servants, "Do whatever he tells you" (John 2:5). Announcing the opportunity, she then steps back to see what Jesus will do. Mary has faithfully carried her perceptions about Him in her heart; now as she releases Him into His destiny, she rests in the sweet assurance that she has faithfully stewarded and now is blessed to see the fulfillment of her calling as Jesus' mother.

> Mary faithfully carried her perceptions about Him in her heart; now she releases Him into His destiny.

Jesus steps up to turn water into wine, going above and beyond to surprise everyone with the very best wine of the party. The apostle John points out how pivotal this moment was for himself and his fellow disciples, having witnessed Jesus' first public miracle. He concludes the account of this miracle by remarking that Jesus "manifested his glory. And his disciples believed in him" (John 2:11).

It was a monumental moment in history and in the lives of Jesus' disciples. I'm sure Jesus could have launched His ministry and stepped into His destiny in some other way, but I love that He allowed us to see what this looks like in the context of a healthy mother-child relationship. This is what it is for a mother to expedite her child into his or her purpose by faithfully discerning times and seasons in her child's life, by recognizing those defining moments when prophecy meets promise. It is an irreplaceable assignment of motherhood and I love that the Lord gives it to His daughters to partner with Him in calling out those moments in our (spiritual and natural) children's lives that propel them into their callings.

Recognizing defining moments when prophecy meets promise is an irreplaceable assignment of motherhood.

Inspiring the Calling

Motherhood is a unique assignment given to women, and I truly believe there are numerous people in each of our lives that God brings to us for spiritual mothering.

Mothering is not the only way women release destiny though. Sometimes we are to bring forth destiny in a different way. This is particularly true when it comes to spiritual leaders, people of influence, and husbands. Although these relationships may require hints of spiritual mothering at times, they primarily need us to manifest our nature as destiny catalysts.

This brings us to the second way women facilitate destiny—through inspiration.

Women are uniquely equipped to inspire, both each other as well as the men in our lives, in ways that are more impactful and far-reaching than most of us realize we are capable of. I think the reason for this is multifaceted but in part related to the way God has specifically gifted women to carry and release destiny. I believe there is something irresistibly inspiring and destiny-releasing when one comes in contact with a woman who is at rest in her own calling and confident in the person God made her to be. That effect is multiplied even further if that woman knows you enough—or perhaps is even perceptive enough without knowing you personally—to be able to see the things the spiritual realm is pregnant with for you, and wait expectantly to release them.

In his book, *Becoming a Leader,* Dr. Myles Munroe wrote that "Inspiration is the key to true leadership". He explains that the goal of leadership is not to produce followers but to inspire followers to become leaders and fulfill their own potential. "To inspire," Dr. Munroe goes on, "is to activate, stimulate, energize, illuminate, motivate by divine influence, or breath into", and it is aimed at enabling others to "discover themselves, their purpose and abilities, and maximize their potential".

> **"Inspiration is the key to true leadership." – Dr. Myles Munroe**

This is why woman's inspiration is so important—to lead is to inspire, and to inspire is to release destiny. God equipped us with innate inspirational capacity unique to the calling and nature of our womanhood.

One woman of the Bible who stewarded well her inspirational power is introduced in the book of 1 Samuel. David, the future king of Israel, has run for his life to escape the jealous rage of the current king, Saul. Living in the wilderness as a vagabond while carrying the heavy and seemingly impossible promise that he would one day be king, he and his men come near the dwelling place of a man by the name of Nabal, and his wife Abigail. In the past, David had treated Nabal's shepherds with respect. Now he comes in peace, sending messengers ahead to respectfully ask for Nabal's support and hospitality.

Nabal, however, has no respect for the prophetic words given over David. In pride he asserts that he will not give David honor as king a day before he assumes the throne. Nabal does not even give David the honor due him as a fellow Hebrew nor even the honor Jewish culture traditionally gave to strangers. God had instructed Israel to care for and support their fellow Jewish people who were in need (Leviticus 25:35) and instructed them to love even strangers as themselves (Leviticus 19:34), yet Nabal shows his future king disdain, arrogantly demanding David first prove himself worthy.

David is angered by Nabal's response, and in many ways, rightfully so. Nabal refuses to display even common courtesy and seemingly goes out of his way to trample on David's dignity during a time of deep vulnerability when David was clinging by a thread to the hope of the promises given to him.

While David is on his way to avenge himself and destroy Nabal, Nabal's "discerning and beautiful" (1 Samuel 25:3) wife Abigail hears of the foolish actions of her husband and takes quick action to intercede on behalf of her family. She hurriedly prepares food for David and his men and goes out to meet him, immediately dismounting to show David honor, and humbly apologizing for the way David was treated. She even goes so far as to offer herself in place of her family: "On me alone, my lord, be the guilt… Please forgive the trespass of your servant." (1 Samuel 25:24, 28).

From this posture of humility, Abigail then goes on to remind David of the prophetic promises made over his life: "The Lord will certainly make my lord a sure house, because my lord is fighting the battles of the Lord... and when the Lord has done to my lord according to all the good that he has spoken concerning you and has appointed you prince over Israel..." (1 Samuel 25:28, 30). She lets him know that she believes in the words spoken over him and she reminds him who he is, thereby igniting the spark that sets him back on course toward his destiny.

David was in a vulnerable place when he came across this wise woman. I believe that women are gifted in a unique way to see the vulnerabilities of the men in their lives because God designed us to be able to take those vulnerabilities and inspire them into strengths. The Enemy and our own selfish hearts like to encourage us to use the vulnerabilities we see for our own advantage to gain the upper hand. However, true leadership is not about raising ourselves up, but about raising others up. True leaders don't aim for followers—instead, they aim to turn followers into leaders, and according to Kingdom rules, the greatest person is the one who is the best at serving. One way we as women are uniquely equipped to lead is through our ability to inspire greatness from brokenness, turn tragedy to triumph, and transform hopeless situations into destiny-releasing encounters.

> **She reminds him who he is, thereby igniting the spark that sets him back on course toward his destiny.**

In her book, *Fight Like a Girl,* author and speaker Lisa Bevere speaks of "the power of feminine virtue and beauty to stir a man to a higher purpose". She writes of the power of woman to inspire fathers to nurture and protect, sons to bestow honor, and brothers to protect their sisters. She likens this aspect of womanhood to an image of a young maiden using a sword to knight a man kneeling in front of her. In her hands, the sword is "no longer a weapon but an instrument of transformation. It is not presented to threaten, wound, or strike the man; it is extended to set him apart. He is no longer the same... With the sword, she transfers the power and confers something only she can give: a higher purpose and reason to live".

The opportunity to inspire often presents itself in someone's moment of deepest vulnerability. In those moments, we can either usurp the last of that person's strength in an attempt to feed our own need for validation, or, if we are coming from a place of security in who God made us to be as women and a healthy respect for the power of that sword we are destined to carry, we can lend our strength to transform those moments of vulnerability into defining moments that ultimately release destiny.

The opportunity to inspire often presents itself in someone's moment of deepest vulnerability.

In my own life, I've often seen the inspirational power of my womanhood on a practical level with my pastors and spiritual leaders. I think it can be easy for us to assume that our leaders are too faith-filled to struggle with doubt or discouragement. We can forget that they are equally human and, in all likelihood, even more targeted by the Enemy than we are because of the positions of authority they carry. I am amazed at the way my pastors and leaders are often so deeply encouraged by a simple word affirming a timely message or acknowledging the call of God on their life. Those moments remind me that inspiration is an effective motivator toward destiny and an important way the Lord specifically equipped women to propel His purposes for the people He has chosen to lead in advancing His Kingdom.

When given such opportunity, Abigail rose to the occasion and exercised well her gift of inspiration. Rather than take advantage of David's hurt and vulnerability, she seized the opportunity to set this future king of Israel back on his path, allowing her destiny to become intertwined with his and ultimately changing history to protect the destiny of one of the most influential men to have ever lived.

Destiny Catalysts

When God gives a word over our lives, we are responsible to not only agree with Him but also partner with Him. God does not override human free will and so often He is just waiting for someone to stand in the gap and partner with Him in what He has declared. "Whom shall I send, and who will go for us?" God asked from His throne room in Isaiah 6:8. Agreeing with God verbally while refusing to partner with Him is like buying a field but then neglecting to do anything with it. As women, we are designed to develop the things we take possession of, to plant vines in that field (Proverbs 31:16), and nurture Holy Spirit fruitfulness out of spiritually barren land.

Using the tool of healed trust and the two methods of mothering and inspiring, women transform prophecy into promise at a rate not naturally possible. The destiny-catalyzing assignment God gave us is a supernatural gift and a weighty and impactful weapon we wield against the Enemy's attempts to disrupt God's plans.

> "Charm is deceptive, and beauty does not last; but a woman who fears the Lord will be greatly praised."
>
> Proverbs 31:30 NLT

Power & Purpose

Putting it All Together

Somewhere along my journey to discover the purpose and power of woman, as I started to believe that being a woman is a *good* thing and something to rejoice in rather than be ashamed of, a good friend of mine likened me to a particular woman of the Bible—Esther.

The comparison surprised me. I hate to admit it, but Esther was not someone I particularly admired—she seemed too feminine (remember that being a woman was not always something I saw as valuable!). However, throughout this journey to discover the way God built women to reflect His strength in a uniquely feminine way, I have come to so admire the woman of strength, boldness, and yes, femininity, that Esther was.

Esther was a woman of power and purpose who exemplified divinely-imparted purity, prayer, peace, perception, provision, protection, and purpose-releasing in order to influence the destiny of a nation and create a legacy. We have already mentioned Esther briefly, but I believe her story deserves specific attention. In this behind-the-scenes glimpse, we see who Esther was, how she brought her unique influence as a woman into the realm of the highest-ranking officials of her time in order to deliver and govern her people with righteousness and justice, and in so doing, how she brought Kingdom values to earth for the benefit of God's people.

From Orphan to Queen

We aren't given many details of Esther's childhood or the circumstances leading to her parents' death but we do know that Esther (Hadassah) was an orphan and was raised by her cousin Mordecai. Her simple life as a Jewish girl living under submission to the Persian empire abruptly ended when the Persian Queen Vashti was removed from her position, having failed in her assignment as leader-influencer. At the suggestion of the king's attendants, a search for a suitable queen begins. As the queen-search gets underway, young Hadassah is among those taken to the king's palace. There her name is changed to Esther and, as mentioned earlier, she is stripped of everything that has ever defined her including her people, her religion, her culture, and even her name. She is then ushered into a twelve-month preparation process—twelve months to adopt her new royal identity, twelve months to become 'queen material'.

I think it's sometimes easy for us to look at great leaders and assume they stepped into their destinies easily, forgetting that there is always a backstory of preparation before that moment of destiny can be released. While I believe the preparation phase is something that we all need to go through in some form in order to mature into the people God designed us to be, I also believe we have a degree of influence over its pace and duration depending on how willingly we submit to the process the Lord wants to take us on.

The women who comprised the king's new harem had equal time to cultivate and take hold of their royal identity, but Esther appears to have jumped headlong into the task right from the start. She quickly wins the favor of the keeper of the women, and in return is given preference and honor, paving the way for her to become best prepared to serve a king and lead a nation. Identity work is hard work. But Esther knew that it was not an accident she had been chosen. It was not a mistake that the God she has served so faithfully would allow her the opportunity to become the most influential woman in the Persian kingdom.

And so she dives into the soul-searching, heart-exploding, hard work of learning and owning her God-ordained calling. She makes herself ready, and when the time comes, people of influence take notice and welcome her onto her stage. "Esther obtained favor in the sight of all who saw her" (Esther 2:15 NKJV) and importantly, her favor-winning impact had the same effect on the highest-ranking person in the kingdom: "The king loved Esther more than all the other women, and she won grace and favor in his sight." (Esther 2:17 NKJV)

> She dives into the soul-searching, hard work of learning and owning her God-ordained calling.

There is something in Esther the king takes note of, a beauty and purity of soul that he is immediately drawn to. He can't resist. Each of the women brought before the king were beautiful. But there was something about Esther, something in her spirit that pulled him in and he just knew. He knew she was the one, that there was no woman who could compare with Esther. The search was over. Esther had changed the spiritual atmosphere in the way only a woman of purity can, and he knew he had found a woman destined to be queen—a woman who understood the unique power and influence of a woman and was at rest in the beautiful person God made her to be. He had found a woman who could lead alongside him, not with the anointing of man, but with the unique destiny-releasing anointing of woman.

King Ahasuerus quickly sees that he made the right decision when only a short time later, Esther exposes a plot against him and saves his life. But Esther is more well known for a plot she mitigated years later, this one with stakes that were much higher. Haman, the king's right-hand man, became bitter when Esther's cousin Mordecai refused to bow down to him and retaliated by manipulating the king into approving a law that would lead to the destruction of the Jewish people. At that point, Mordecai sends word to Esther and Esther realizes she is the only one in the entire kingdom with the ability to influence the king and protect her people. Only the king outranks Haman, and Esther is the only one who can possibly exert more influence over the king than Haman does.

Esther considers the weight of the call and prepares herself accordingly. She spends three days in fasting and prayer, inviting her family to join in spiritual solidarity and leading the women in her sphere of influence to do the same. During this time of soul-searching prayer, Esther ultimately determines she is willing to die for the sake of her people. There is nothing weak about the influence of a powerful woman. Esther knew what was at stake. Like any good leader, she counted the cost ahead of time and knew she was willing to pay the highest price to realize her destiny and save her nation. Provers 31:10 says that "a woman who fears the Lord will be greatly praised." The fear of the Lord is not truly tested until it comes head-to-head with the fear of man. Esther feared the Lord more than she feared any man and therefore the rules of an earthly king could not compare to the command of her heavenly King. Long before she received the call to defend her people before the Persian king, Esther's mind was made up to follow God's lead no matter the cost.

The fear of the Lord is not truly tested until it comes head-to-head with the fear of man.

Armed with the assurance that this was her time, her call, and her responsibility whatever the outcome, Esther dressed for court and came confidently before the king, and "when the king saw Queen Esther standing in the court, she won favor in his sight" (Esther 5:2). The king looks at her; I imagine him locking eyes with her and seeing deep into her soul. She has broken the rules, but he sees the purity and wisdom in her eyes, and he knows she wouldn't be standing there unless she was carrying something worth the cost. As he looks into her eyes, he sees a woman of influence. He recognizes the purity of heart and the power of woman she carries, and he accepts her bold move.

God designed women to reflect His beauty and purity, to demonstrate different aspects of His nature than those men are uniquely equipped to carry. In our culture, beauty is often misunderstood. We can be tempted to either overvalue it, making it everything, or undervalue it. Personally, I have often erred on the side of undervaluing beauty. Fear of unwanted attention made me run from my unique identity as a woman. But I am learning that the power lies more with me as the receiver, and that when and *how* I receive the way people take notice of me can open (or close) doors to my unique influence as a woman.

> **God's deep, spiritual beauty has a way of capturing hearts, inspiring willpower, and activating dreams in a way nothing else on earth can.**

It also changed my mindset to realize that God created beauty in His daughters and in the world in general, not so we could exploit beauty or serve the idol of people-pleasing, but that we might be a reflection of His nature.

God's beauty—His deep, spiritual beauty—has a way of capturing hearts, inspiring willpower, and activating dreams in a way nothing else on earth can, and He designed women to reflect this beauty in a way that gives us unique influence in the world. The beauty and purity of soul within us were designed to inspire the men in our lives to be better men, motivate leaders to operate in purity, and ground the Church in the beauty of God's holiness.

In Proverbs 31, Solomon concludes his description of a godly woman by saying: "[Superficial] beauty is vain, but a woman who fears the Lord [reverently worshiping, obeying, serving, and trusting Him with awe-filled respect], she shall be praised. Give her of the product of her hands, and let her own works praise her in the gates [of the city]" (Proverbs 31:30-31 AMP).

Esther's beauty went far beyond the superficial level, reaching the deepest places of her heart, and attuning her soul and spirit to seek only the Lord. When it came to choosing between people's opinion and God's opinion, she refused to be swayed by the pressure to conform, even when it was the king of the Persian Empire she had to stand before in order to follow God's lead. Esther operated from a heart of purity, motivated solely by her love for God, and that purity of heart was something the people around her took notice of and were inspired by.

It was in this way that Esther released the destiny of her husband-king and protected the future of an entire people and nation. The task at hand—the salvation of her family and the Jewish people—depended on her ability to own her place as a woman of influence. She carried the assignment well, earning the praise worthy of a woman whose actions reflected her courageous decision to live her life in the fear of the Lord.

A Woman of Purity

Esther had spent time cultivating and developing purity as her identity, until purity was more than simply a quality she possessed—it became a part of *who* she was by nature, motivating her desires, dreams, and bold actions. With that foundation, all Esther had to do was walk into the room and people paid attention. She carried something within her that captivated the attention of those around her and ultimately changed the fate of an entire nation.

Our King is drawn to purity in this same way. He can't resist it. Purity is the atmosphere of heaven. And when we carry that atmosphere within us, heaven naturally invades that space because God inhabits holiness. When the tabernacle in the wilderness was purified and prepared for Him, God showed up. When Solomon dedicated and purified the temple, God showed up. And when our hearts are purified before Him, He shows up. He comes in, inhabits, dwells, makes Himself at home. A woman carrying the purity of heart that attracts and invites the presence of the Living God is irresistible to those attuned to the deep beauty of holiness, and will invariably activate divine destiny for those willing to receive the purity-inspired influence a woman carries.

A Woman of Prayer

I believe that in addition to being a woman of purity, Esther was a woman of prayer. Personally, I think the time of fasting and prayer she set aside before stepping into her destiny was not a one-time event. Rather, it was an expression of a lifestyle of prayer developed over years of depending on her God through times of tragedy after her parents died and times of uncertainty as she was whisked away to be the potential bride of a pagan king. I believe that fasting before her assignment was a natural response for her because she had cultivated a lifestyle of prayer and fasting. Queen Esther made her dwelling in the secret place with God.

A Woman of Peace

Esther's deep communion with her God prepared her for what was perhaps the most important piece needed for her to complete her task—surrender to her true King. Peace requires surrender, and in order to obtain the boldness to carry out her assignment in the fearless way she did, Esther needed to come to the place of full surrender in which she could boldly say, "I will go to the king, though it is against the law, and if I perish, I perish" (Esther 4:16).

Surrender opens doors in ways nothing else can. Esther's surrender opened the door to rescue her people from destruction. Jesus' surrender opened the door to salvation, redemption, and restoration, and God still opens doors through our surrender. Surrender is the scariest thing the Lord asks us to do, but it is also the most rewarding. And it seems the higher the stakes (such as entrusting Him with the lives of ourselves and our loved ones, as in Esther's case), the greater the reward. There is no person or situation the Lord doesn't have a right to ask from us, and yet as a good Father, He only asks so that He can pour out exceedingly more than we could ever obtain through our own imaginations and human capabilities (Ephesians 3:20). As the gentleman He is, He never forces His way in, but He does stand at the door and knock (Revelation 3:20), seeking for those who are willing to lose their life in order to find it (Matthew 16:25), and inviting us to have life and have it more abundantly (John 10:10).

Surrender opens doors in ways nothing else can.

A Woman of Perception

In all her proceedings, Esther acted with wisdom. She was discreet, asking humbly for a private audience with the king and Haman, rather than publicly shaming him that first day she walked into court. She then continued to evaluate the unfolding situation day by day and responded in wisdom accordingly. If I were in her shoes, I am sure I would have felt the pressure rising and I'm not sure I could have kept from prematurely spilling the beans! But Esther was patient and followed God's timing, feeling out the situation for the opportune moment. At banquet number one, she discerned that the time was not right and deferred her request until a second banquet, denying her need to vindicate herself and subjecting herself to another day of serving the man who planned to commit genocide against her people. Her patience in waiting on God's timing provided the opportunity for the king to have a divine dream, reminding him of the way Mordecai had saved his life and prompting him to command Haman to honor Mordecai the following day. It was very likely this twenty-four hour delay that allowed God the time to work in the king's heart and open the door for Esther to speak and propel him to act on her behalf.

> She continued to evaluate the unfolding situation day by day and responded in wisdom accordingly.

Proverbs 9:10 (NLT) says, "Fear of the Lord is the foundation of wisdom. Knowledge of the Holy One results in good judgment." Esther's life exemplified the fear of the Lord. She acted, not in accordance with her own fears or insecurities, but with wisdom that could only come from above, giving her divine revelation so she could work in partnership with God to save her people.

A Woman of Provision

Esther provided for her family (as demonstrated by her bringing Mordecai clothing when she thought he was in need), for those she hosted (as demonstrated by her banquets), and more importantly, through her spiritual leadership. Before stepping into an assignment that had the potential to change the fate of a nation, Esther didn't pray and fast alone; instead, she led the women whom the king had given her, as well as the entire Jewish population of Susa, to fast and pray with her. I find it remarkable that the women of the palace apparently had no qualms about giving up food for three days to come into spiritual agreement with a queen whose allegiance was to Yahweh, the God of the minority Jewish people. I am convinced that these women saw in Esther what the king saw in her—the beauty of holiness that attracted them to want to know more about this God she served. Of all the things Esther provided, the fear of the Lord and her wisdom and kindness (see Proverbs 31:26) were the most important provisions she made as leader of her people and Queen of Persia.

A Woman of Prophetic Destiny

Finally, at a banquet with the king and Haman, Esther made her request. Pouring out her heart, she beseeched the king with tears on behalf of her people. The king was immediately impacted. He saw her heart in that moment, and the strength and purity of her bold request caused him to spring into action. He responded by fiercely protecting her and her family and then he went on to do even more, promoting her family to honor. The king trusted Esther because she was pure of heart and fiercely committed to her people and her call, and as a result, he was willing to do anything for her.

She was pure of heart and fiercely committed to her people and her call.

That is the natural response to the destiny-releasing, world-changing purity of heart God designed women to carry. At that moment, Esther released destiny for herself, her husband-king, and her entire nation.

A Woman of Protection

The account of Esther's rescue of her family and her people from Haman's planned massacre ends with the inauguration of an annual holiday of remembrance, a commemoration of the reversal of a decree that had been meant to destroy the Jewish people and instead was used to destroy their enemies.

But Esther's protection of her people didn't end there. This story was just the beginning of her stepping into her call. From that moment on, Esther walked out as the leader she was always destined to be, ruling alongside her husband and continuing to advocate for her people. Years later, in the twentieth year of his reign (Nehemiah 2:1),

King Ahasuerus (also known as Artaxerxes) receives another request regarding the Jewish people. As the request pertains to the Jews, it assuredly leads him to reflect back on Esther's rise to leadership through sacrificial protection of her people in response to his near-destruction of the Jews.

Queens were not regular attendees of judicial proceedings, yet the Scripture tells us that Queen Esther was in attendance for this particular request. Evidently, after reflecting on how nearly he had been deceived, and how faithful Queen Esther's leadership had been over the many years since that day she stepped up to reverse the plot against the Jews, he determines that his Queen should sit beside him in this important meeting regarding the Jewish people. This time, it is Nehemiah, the cupbearer to the king, who prayerfully approaches the king and makes his request. Nehemiah wishes to return to Jerusalem and build a wall of protection around the city in response to God's call. Then he, Nehemiah, records the king's response: "The king said to me (the queen sitting beside him), 'How long will you be gone, and when will you return?'" (Nehemiah 2:6).

I can only imagine the unrecorded discussion, perhaps even the nonverbal discussion, that took place between King Ahasuerus and Queen Esther in the moment before the king gave his reply to Nehemiah. Whatever she said verbally, I am sure her eyes told him, "Say yes."

Not only did the king allow Nehemiah to make his journey and take whatever time he needed, but he went much further, sending him with an escort of army officers for protection and letters of permission to secure the lumber needed for the work. Nehemiah repeatedly acknowledged the good hand of his God upon him, and I am sure Queen Esther, a woman endowed with divine favor herself, was instrumental in imparting to Nehemiah the divine favor he needed for his task of securing continued protection for her people.

Power and Purpose

As a woman of influence, Esther carried herself with grace and dignity. She was unafraid and untamed, yet elegant and receptive, wise and discreet. Esther released the destinies of kings and nations through her unique and powerful influence as a woman. We as women are designed by the Father with that same destiny-releasing capacity to influence and facilitate the things He dreamt up and entrusted us to carry.

Woman, allow me to introduce you to you: You are a container for God's purity, a partner of the living God through prayer, a resting place for God's peace, a communicator of divine wisdom, a provider of firm foundations, protector of your spiritual family, and a releaser of divine destiny.

Your Enemy is afraid of you finding out who you are and taking possession of the spiritual land you were destined to inhabit. But the gig is up; we've called the devil on his lies, and we are ready to occupy our land and own our identities as the women of power and purpose God sees us to be.

The world is waiting for the King's daughters to rise up, to recognize the Queens we are, and step into our place of power and purpose. Let's not make the world wait any longer. It is time for us to take our place.

The task God assigned you to carry out and the place God assigned you to be could only be accomplished through the specific qualities He put inside of His marvelous creation called woman.

You were created to be powerful.

You were created to drive back darkness.

You were created to shine the pure light of His presence.

You were created to anchor families and nations in God's goodness.

You were created for now, for such a time as this.

You were created for places of honor and praise.

> "This virtuous woman lives in the wonder, awe, and fear of the Lord. She will be praised throughout eternity."
>
> Proverbs 31:30 TPT

Woman, welcome to your place.

Epilogue

I hope through this journey, you are encouraged to believe for the woman of power and purpose God sees you to be. God made women on purpose and He had incredible things in His heart for us even before the first woman came into being.

I am so thankful for the ways the Lord has been taking me on a journey with Him to rebuke the lies the devil has spoken over my life, restoring me to embrace my identity as a woman and as a daughter of the King. There is no freedom that compares to the freedom that comes from breaking agreement with a lie. I love the sweet freedom in Jesus. The Lord has set me free from so many things this past year and I know He set me free in part so that I could partner with Him to set others free too. Women of the Kingdom, here is your invitation to freedom—your invitation to break agreement with the lies of the Enemy so you can walk out the callings and destinies on your life, experiencing the peaceful confidence of a woman who knows her identity, knows her God, and knows how to take captive every lie to stand on the unshakeable foundation of truth.

God created women to be vessels of His purity, prayer partners of His Spirit, resting places of His peace, messengers of His perceptions, providers of His foundations, protectors of His families, and releasers of His destinies. His design for woman was always to equip her to be a powerful force, driving back darkness and propelling His marvelous Kingdom of Light in the unique way that is distinctly that of a woman.

I believe in this season we as women are rising to embrace our true identities in Him. I pray that as the truth of your identity washes over you, you would experience ever increasing levels of the freedom Jesus won for you, going from glory heights to glory heights in the Kingdom that knows no bounds. He is the God of the infinite and the impossible and He sees so much more for us than we see for ourselves. He is the God of "exceedingly abundantly above all we ask or think" (Ephesians 3:20 NKJV). May we see ourselves through the eyes of that God.

May He heal and restore and rebuild you in all the ways you need Him to, and may He impart a double portion of the spirit of wisdom as you cling to His truth. The shame and condemnation and hurt of the past are buried at the foot of the cross and from hereon we step into the newness of life He has had in store all along. Truth is stronger than lie, redemption is stronger than shame, love is stronger than fear, and I pray that for each one of us, this conversation we start with Him never stops.

May the love of the Father, the grace of Jesus, and the sweet friendship of the Holy Spirit fill you to abundance over and over for all of eternity until you abound with all the fullness of God.

References

Brown, Francis, Driver, S. R., Briggs, Charles A. (1996). The Brown-Driver-Briggs Hebrew and English Lexicon. Peabody, MA: Hendrickson Publishers.

Hicks, Bethany. (2019). Own Your Assignment: Every Woman's Call to Raise Up World Changers.

Munroe, Myles. (1993). Becoming a Leader: Everyone Can Do It. Lanham, MD: Pneuma Life Publishing.

Bevere, Lisa. (2006). Fight Like a Girl. New York, NY: FaithWords, Hachette Book Group USA.

Carmichael, A. (2010). Thou Givest… They Gather: Truths gleaned from the Word of God. Washington, PA: CLC Publications.

Vine, W.E., Unger, M. F., White, W. (1996). Vine's Complete Expository Dictionary of Old and New Testament Words. Thomas Nelson, Inc. (Original work published 1985).

Bevere, John. (2020). X: Multiply Your God-Given Potential. Palmer Lake, CO: Messenger International.

McCollam, Dan. (2016). Prophetic Company: the joyful journey toward building prophetic community. Vacaville, CA: Sounds of the Nations.

www.ingramcontent.com/pod-product-compliance
Lightning Source LLC
Chambersburg PA
CBHW030259010526
44107CB00053B/1760